MW00779175

My Life Before

A Memoir of a Family
Created Through Adoption

By Andry & Pippa Seichrist

Copyright © 2024 Andry & Pippa Seichrist

All rights reserved. ISBN: 979-8-89324-384-0

Printed in the United States of America.

No part of this publication shall be reproduced, transmitted, or sold in whole or in part in any form without the prior written consent of the author, except as provided by the United States of America copyright law. Any unauthorized usage of the text without express written permission of the publisher is a violation of the author's copyright and is illegal and punishable by law. All trademarks and registered trademarks appearing in this guide are the property of their respective owners.

The opinions expressed by the Author are not necessarily those held by the Publishers.

The information contained within this book is strictly for informational purposes. The material may include information, products, or services by third parties. As such, the Author and Publisher do not assume responsibility or liability for any third-party material or opinions. The publisher is not responsible for websites (or their content) that are not owned by the publisher. Readers are advised to do their own due diligence when it comes to making decisions.

Dedication

This book is dedicated to all the people who are considering adopting an older child.

Andry, Olya and me in the Carpathian Mountains in 2006. We spent a week sightseeing in the mountains, while we waited for our court date to finalize Andry's adoption.

Contents

Prologue

I felt the infant's sharp teeth dig into my shoulder. Startled by the pain, my hands flew up, and the little bundle I had been holding fell to the ground. I stared as the blanket wriggled, and a rabbit peeked out and hopped away.

That was the odd, recurring dream I had during my freshman year of college. Once I figured out what it meant, I never had the dream again. I realized that through the dream, I was telling myself to lead an unexpected life. (The idea of living in a house in the suburbs with a white picket fence had always made me feel trapped.) I had no idea what my future would be, but I knew I wanted it to be an adventure.

A few years after grad school, I married a man who proposed to me 127 times before I said "yes." He actually asked me to marry him before we even had our first date. The proposals came in long, beautifully written letters that made me cry, in cartoons he drew that made me laugh, and taped to the chest of an inflatable gorilla. Ron proposed in a fish pet store in Atlanta during the sunset performance of the opera La Boheme in Santa Fe, New Mexico, and over a candlelit dinner he cooked at his house. His proposals were all as unique and creative as he is. Thank goodness he was persistent!

Over the next 30 years, Ron and I worked together every day in the business we started together. We founded the school we wish we could have gone to. The school trained young people for careers in advertising and design. The single school we started in Miami with six students grew to have locations in 14 cities in eight countries. Our graduates have been very successful. If you've watched a Super Bowl since the mid-90s, you've seen their commercials because every year, a few spots, usually the funniest ones, are done by our graduates.

Ron and I traveled all over the U.S., Europe, and Latin America. We met with the presidents of companies, spoke at big conferences, and became friends with fascinating people. Somewhere in the middle of all that, we realized our life together was so special that we needed to share it with a child. Most people want to adopt a baby, but we decided to adopt an older girl. Older children are not likely to be adopted and often face a bleak life. Becoming adoptive parents began the most remarkable chapter of our lives.

Pippa and Ron Seichrist in Miami around 2007.

1. What's the First Thing You Remember?

(Pippa's story)

Ron, Olya, the little girl we had adopted five years earlier, and I had been home with Andry for three months. Officially, he was our son, but we still knew so little about him. What had his life been like back in Ukraine?

Andry acted terrible sometimes. His reactions didn't make sense to me or Ron or even Olya, his biological little sister. Often, we wondered why he was moody or upset for no apparent reason, but we couldn't ask him. Even though he was almost fourteen and just a few inches shorter than me, conversations with him, because of his limited vocabulary, were the kind you would have with a toddler, just basic statements, questions, and directions like "It's cold," "Are you hungry?" or "Let's go now." I was slowly learning a few things about him. He didn't like peanut butter, he loved to ride bikes, and he always wanted to arm wrestle, but he hadn't yet been able to discuss thoughts or feelings. Fortunately, he was learning English faster than we had imagined possible.

I had just finished making cornbread dressing, my grandmother's recipe with chopped scallions and chicken broth, when Ron came in to start preparing oyster dressing from his family's recipe. The next day was Thanksgiving, and Ron and I always filled the table with our favorite dishes we had eaten when we were growing up. For the last 18 years, we had spent Thanksgiving at our vacation house, a turn-of-the-century farmhouse we had bought right after we got married and restored. We always invited

1

lots of people for the holiday: my parents, Ron's grown children, and their families, students, and friends. Between the people and the dogs, cats, horses, donkeys, and ducks, there was a lot going on.

Even though Andry often acted angry, I knew he liked us because he would seek out our company. While I was cooking, he had brought his computer into the kitchen and sat at the table near me to play video games, calling me over to see when he was successful at killing the alien or squashing the tomato. As Ron washed his hands, getting ready for his turn in the kitchen, he asked Andry, "Want to help me cook?" Ron had learned how to cook from his father and thought it would be something special to share with his new son. When Andry got up to mix the corn, oysters, and bread crumbs together, I took his seat at the table. I sat thinking and watching the two of them together. I wondered what Andry had been like as a little boy and what people and life experiences had shaped him.

As Andry helped Ron put the dressing and apples in the turkey, I asked him, "What's the first thing you remember?" I didn't know if Andry would understand my question or if he would have enough words to express himself, but the moment seemed right. Andry started to talk. After only a few sentences, I knew I had to save his words. The way they flowed off of his memory was unexpected and amazing. I spun his computer around and started transcribing the story he told us about hopelessness and stealing his best friend's scooter in the middle of the night. When Andry finished, I showed him what I had typed. He smiled. It was clear he had liked telling us about his life. He had liked the attention. I asked, "Do you want to tell me another story tomorrow?"

That's how this book started. Andry and I wrote most of these stories at a coffee shop on Saturday mornings.

2. The Scooter

(Andry's story)

I had three friends. One of them, Sasha, was rich at that time, with a big house, tractors, and all different types of vehicles. To go to his house, you had to go straight and then high up the hill and to the right. Sasha had a scooter. Before school, I asked if I could have it, but he said, "No." His father had given it to him. I stole his scooter that winter night.

It was during the day that I decided to steal the scooter. While in school, I thought about how to do it, drawing my plan on blank papers while the teacher talked. Without a plan, things can go wrong. During the day, Sasha's mother was always working next to the house, putting out laundry on the lines and feeding chickens. I knew night would be the best time because everyone would be sleeping. If you want to steal something, the best way is to do it at night or during the day when no one is home. At night, you have to be careful because people have guns. I knew Sasha's father had a gun because he went hunting. He could shoot at a shape without looking at the face.

After school, Sasha went back to his house, and I went my way. He was a good friend. When it was cold, and I didn't have food, he brought me some, a big fish called *karas*, which means carp in Ukrainian. The night comes early in winter. I stayed up and didn't go to sleep. I went to his house. He had a fat, sweet Rottweiler. The dog knew me. I gave him a piece of bread, and while he was eating, I took the scooter. I got it and started running. I was so happy. A light in the house came on, but I was, by that time, many houses away.

In the village where I was born, there are four different colors. Spring is gray because the water is running on the streets. During summer, everything is so green that it almost seems unreal. In autumn, the village is yellow and orange but mostly orange. And in the winter, it is pure white like the sheets I have on my bed now. Then, it was winter, and I couldn't use the scooter. It had three wheels and a seat and couldn't roll in the snow.

Sasha didn't realize until spring that his scooter was gone. He asked me if I knew where it was. Then there were questions like, "Do you want to go to your house to look for it?" I would say, "I am your friend. I would never do that." I had no feelings in that life. Now, I can say how sad that was.

One time, when no one was at the hill where we usually played, I took the scooter to ride. My friend was hiding behind a tree and came out. He said, "I knew you took it. Give it back." I didn't even feel ashamed when he took his scooter back. We stayed friends, but he didn't trust me so much. I was never invited inside his house again. I had to wait outside. I didn't care. I didn't have anything and didn't care about anything.

In Ukraine, everyone is poor. In the beginning, people try to do something with their lives, but it never works. They give up and drink. If you don't have anything, it's easier to be drunk.

These little boys in the village are the same age I was when
I stole my friend's scooter one winter night.

3. The Hat

(Andry's story)

When Maria and Nikolai, my biological parents, were working, Maria would wake me up, and there would be milk and bread with jelly, butter, or wet bread with sugar. I would walk alone to school, it wasn't far. Classes lasted from morning to afternoon. In school, my teachers never encouraged me to learn. I don't think they expected much from me because of the family I came from.

I was always tired in school because I stayed up late to explore and steal at night. Maria didn't know I was going out at night but even if she had known I don't think she would have said anything.

I liked kindergarten because they fed us mannaya kasha, a porridge made of semolina, sugar, salt, and milk, but I hated naptime after we ate. Naps were for little kids, and I was already past that. I had to do things to explore. I would say, "Can I go to the toilet?" which was outside, behind the school. I didn't actually go. I would climb the fence and leave. Other times, I couldn't leave because the teacher would be watching, so I would hide under one of the playground slides. One time, I was hiding behind the slide, and the teacher was looking for me. I was scared because if she caught me, she would get my ear. After she left, I ran for my life and wandered around the village.

I remember that in first grade, the teacher read the class a book called Bukvar, or alphabet book. I guess we were studying the letter Z because the animal's name was Zayets, which means rabbit. The story was about a rabbit that goes outside in the winter. I remember looking at the picture for a long time. There was a grass hill with a rabbit on top. The story compares a wild rabbit and another type of rabbit, a Krol, which is a huge, gray domestic rabbit. One turns white in wintertime; the krol stays gray.

In school, there were three classes: reading, math, and gym. In gym class, there was a rope tied to the ceiling that the kids would climb up as an exercise. I climbed up but was too scared to climb down. The teacher yelled at me, "Andry, get down!" It was cold in the gym, and I was wearing a hat. As I figured out how to get down the rope, my hat fell on the floor. In my rush to do what the teacher had said, I forgot about my hat and went home.

At home, my little sister and brother, Olya and Dima, were taking a nap. Maria was at work so she couldn't tell me what to do. Only Hannah, my babusha grandmother, was home, but I mostly ignored her. I dropped off my book bag. I didn't change because I didn't have any other clothes. I went fishing. Sometimes, we would eat the fish I caught unless they were too small.

When I got home, it was very late, but Maria made me do my homework because I had played during the day. The house had three rooms and was dark and cold. There wasn't electricity, so I sat at the table doing my math worksheet by candlelight. That was the only source of light. I remember looking at the problem for a long time as if I would just see the answer: 7 - 5 = ___. I couldn't figure out what the solution was. It was easy to go up on my fingers, but going down was hard.

The next day was windy and even colder. While I was walking to school, the mayor stopped his car and asked, "Where is your hat?" I said it was at the school gym. He said, "Let's go to the school to get it." Then he drove me to Tetiiv, which was about 15 minutes away from the village, in his gray Jetta,

When we got to Tetiiv, I saw Olya and Dima in the back seat of a big van. They were looking out the rear window at me. The mayor took my hand, led me to where the driver was standing, and gave my hand to him. The mayor told him, "It's okay to take them now." As the driver and I walked to the van where Olya and Dima were, he asked me how I was doing in school. I don't remember what I replied.

When we were leaving, I saw Maria. She was standing in front of a huge building with a wooden door. To the right of the door was a sign that said Derzhavniy, government building. She looked skinny and gray like the trees that lined the road on the way from Telizhentsy to Titiiv. She was crying. The van took us to the orphanage.

This is the road from Telizhyntsi, the village the children lived in, to Tetiev, the closest town. The trip takes about 15 minutes by car. Most of the people in the village don't have cars, so the trip takes two hours on foot.

4. Nine Months

(Pippa's story)

Nine months from the day we started filling out the Ukrainian adoption application, we were approved and on a plane to Ukraine to find our little girl. How ironic that giving birth to a child would have taken the same amount of time. Ron and I spent most of the ten-hour flight to Ukraine wondering what our daughter would be like. Would she be outgoing or shy, artistic or athletic, funny or introspective? Would she like animals? We hoped so since we had a big, brown, lovable lab named Smudge and four horses.

Our trip to Ukraine had been delayed by several months because The Department of Homeland Security, which gives adopted children citizenship as soon as their feet touch U.S. soil, had lost our FedExed application. I had to order, once again, a copy of our home study from our adoption agent, a background check from the FBI, original birth certificates from Texas and Virginia, and a marriage license from Colorado.

Ron and I channeled our frustration and spent the extra time preparing our daughter's room. We built a child-size table and chairs out of walnut with maple inlay. Ron had come up with a unique way of embedding magnets in the top of the table with a thin layer of wood covering them. I sculpted toys, also with magnets embedded, that could be attached to the table. One of the toys consisted of two wooden slices of bread that connected with magnets. From colored pieces of felt, I cut Swiss cheese, ham, tomato, and mustard that could be layered between the slices of wooden bread and then stuck to the table. As our trip got delayed longer, I had time to make more and more toys. There was an ice cream cone, an orange slice, a cupcake, a brown lab, a teddy bear, a butterfly, a cat, a ladybug, and a slice of birthday cake. A friend, the owner of Genius Jones, a high-end children's store, saw the furniture and asked Ron to manufacture a line of children's furniture for his store, but we weren't interested. We had been inspired to make the table and chairs for our daughter. We took pictures of the furniture, her room, our house, Smudge, and my parents (who would be her grandparents) and made a photo book to show her what her life would look like in our family.

When Ron and I finally landed in Ukraine, Alex, our adoption facilitator, met us at the airport with bad news. Interpol had seized a suspicious container, and in it was our dossier, including the long-awaited approval from the Department of Homeland Security. These papers were required for our appointment at the adoption center in Kiev. Interpol could take a week, a month, or longer to release the contents of the container. Ron and I were devastated, but there wasn't anything we could do except wait and hope. We decided if Interpol didn't release our papers by the end of the week, we would go home. We couldn't put our lives on hold and wait in Ukraine indefinitely.

As a whole, Ukrainians don't smile. The people on the street and in shops look like they're mad at you. It's unnerving. If you smile at them, they don't return the smile. They just ignore you harder. Pasha and Alla, the Ukrainian couple that Ron and I were staying with, explained that Ukrainians are suspicious of strangers who smile at them. (Our hosts had noticed that Americans are always smiling and wondered if it made our cheeks hurt.)

As unfriendly as Ukrainians seem at first, once you get to know them, they are exceptionally warm and generous. To help us keep our minds off of our missing paperwork, Pasha and Alla spent the week thinking of interesting places to take us. We visited the folk art museum, gold-roofed churches, Andriivska Street, where craftsmen sell souvenirs, and the WWII memorial, Lady Victory, a giant silver-colored statue of a woman, bigger

9

than the Statue of Liberty commemorating victory over the Germans. The bloodiest battle and turning point of the war was the Battle of Kiev. Still hopeful for a successful adoption, we wondered how our future daughter's ancestors had been affected by the war.

Pasha saved the best excursion for last, The Ukrainian Village. Acres of rolling hills were covered in traditional farmhouses. Depending on the region, the small houses were white or yellow ochre with flowers painted around the doors and thatched roofs. At the center of each house was a huge stucco stove with a small metal door at the bottom of one end where wood would be inserted. The most unusual feature of the stove was the long built-in ledge that was stacked with blankets and used as a bed. I wondered how many Ukrainians had woken up on fire!

Workers at the park dressed in traditional Ukrainian costumes and were sprinkled around in exhibits demonstrating pottery, candle making, pansky (egg decorating), and horsemanship. A young woman on the stable staff was rigging horses to a wagon when one slipped away from her. The woman, shrieking and waving a switch in the air, chased the poor critter all over the open fields. Ron and I could have quickly caught the horse for her by letting him settle and then slowly meandering to him with soothing words and a treat. Instead, we silently cheered for the horse...run away, run away, faster! Why would the horse want to come back to her?! She was just going to beat him. What a miserable life he had with her as his caregiver. We wondered if she was just inexperienced or if we would discover that her attitude was common in Ukraine.

My phone rang. It was Alex, our facilitator. Ron, realizing that this was the call we had been waiting for, videotaped me on the phone as tears streamed down my face. Our papers had arrived at the adoption center. Our appointment was the next day!

Ron, Smudge, our dog, and me, with the table we made for our future daughter.

Pasha, Alla, Ron and me at the historical Ukrainian village.

5. Learning to Ask

(Andry's story)

When I was little, our clothes and shoes and everything else were second-hand. We didn't have a refrigerator. Hannah's sister, Hallah, was living in a two-bedroom apartment in Kiev with her son, daughter, their spouses, and one grandson. With five adults in the apartment, who were all working, they could afford new things sometimes. When they got a new refrigerator, we got their old one.

Before the refrigerator, food was kept in drawers, and we would eat it right away or the next morning. We would store stuff that could be stored, but I don't remember having a lot of food in the house, just jars of jam, soft tomatoes, and pickles. These things were kept in the same place the potatoes were stored, in a hole hidden under a section of boards that made the living room floor.

Maria would buy or ask the neighbors for fresh milk for us. We had to be careful not to go to the same neighbor too often. They wouldn't give the milk to her unless she said it was for the kids. I would usually go with her because if they saw me, they were less likely to say "NO." I was only five, but I knew my purpose. I didn't do anything but stand there, smile, and be polite.

In the morning, the cows went to the pasture behind the village. In the evening, when the herd comes home, walking down the main streets in the village, everyone who has a cow stands by their gate and gets their cow when she walks by. After they get the cow, they milk her. That's when

Maria and I would go ask for milk. The milk would be so fresh it was still warm. You could still see the foam on top from being squeezed out of the cow.

When the old ladies didn't want to give the milk because they had just milked the cow and didn't want to do it again, they would tell Maria to go milk the cow herself. We would bring our own glass jar with a lid. That way, people wouldn't have to give us milk and a jar. It's awkward enough to have to ask for the milk. We didn't want to have to ask for a jar, too. Then, we would have to return the jar, reminding them that we had just begged them a couple of days before. We knew they didn't want to see us again.

Sometimes, they wouldn't answer the door. Or people would have excuses like, "My cow didn't give a lot of milk." Some people would say in kind of a rude way, "I don't have any milk," but we knew they did because they had a cow. Maria didn't take it in a bad way. We knew we were a bother in the village, and they didn't want to see us anyway. On another day, she would ask a different neighbor. You don't want to constantly be asking the same person. We weren't the borrowers. We were the beggars. When you borrow, you give back.

A woman in the village walking her cow home.

6. Five-Finger Bookmark

(Pippa's story)

We would have 15 minutes at the adoption center in Kiev to review the binder of available girls and select one to be our daughter. Then we could travel to her region, meet her, and spend a few days playing with her to see if we were right for each other. If, for some reason, she wasn't a match, we could request another session at the adoption center and select another little girl to meet.

We were told that at the age of 17, children age out of the orphanage and must leave. Most spend part of the $20 the orphanage gives them on a bus ticket to the town of some relative in hopes of being taken in. Pimps, knowing girls are released from school at the beginning of the summer, hang out at the bus station befriending the girls and offering them "jobs." We heard that over 20% of the girls turn to prostitution. Twenty percent of the boys wind up in prison, and 10% commit suicide. Their futures are bleak.

When our turn came, we walked into a room with a desk in the middle. Irina, our translator, explained to the expressionless official at the desk that we were hoping for a little girl aged 4-7. The three-ring binder of older girls was brought in for us to look at. Our translator, aware of the time limit, quickly looked through the girls' profile pages, which included their name, age, region, health information, and a passport-sized photo on the top right corner of each page. As she flipped each page, she said, "No, no, no..." Ron and I sat frozen, not knowing what to do. I had talked to a few other people who had adopted older children. They said when they saw their child, they just knew. I was skeptical. How were we going to pick a daughter based on a little photo and a few facts?

Irina explained that she had rejected the girls who were already teenagers, had serious health issues, or had brothers and sisters because that would require us to adopt the entire sibling group because Ukrainian law said the children couldn't be separated. As she continued through the four-inch thick binder, Ron put his hand in the middle of one little girl's page and said, "Tell us about her." Irina said, "No, she has two brothers; one's been adopted," and turned the page with Ron's hand still awkwardly bookmarking the little girl's page. As Irina skimmed more profiles, Ron and I wondered why she wasn't available since the kids had already been separated. He told me, "There is something about the look in her eye that reminds me of you. She's the one." He pushed the book back open to the little girl's page and asked Irina, "What's her name?" Irina said, "Olga." Ron looked at me, laughed, and said, "She IS the one."

Before we left for Ukraine, I started researching "Ukrainian girl names." When I searched on Google, it always led me to a long selection of mail-order bride sites where I would look at the names on the women's profiles, wondering what our daughter's name would be. Since we were adopting an older girl, she would already have a name and identify herself with it. We felt if we changed her name, we would be sending her the message, "We don't accept you for who you are. We want you to be a different person." We didn't want to change Katarina into a Jennifer or Iliana into a Susan. Out of all the names that I found, there was only one that I just couldn't adjust to, and it was Olga.

Irina read Olga's profile to us. She had two brothers. One had been adopted. The other was still in an orphanage but not eligible for adoption. That probably made it possible for us to adopt her. But there was a problem. Olga's profile said she didn't speak. That didn't make any sense to Ron and me. Children talk. Maybe she was shy, or maybe she stuttered. Irina called Olga's orphanage and asked for permission to visit Olga.

7. Just Forget

(Andry's story)

I don't recall Maria ever getting mad or being strict with me. She never punished me. When I told her I stole something while I was at the orphanage, she didn't care. I would tell her to show off that I had something cool, like a new backpack. Something in a store had to impress me for me to steal it.

Once, Nikolai stole a bag of wheat. There was a hole in the bag, and his trail of wheat made a straight line down the road and ended at our house. Didn't he realize that the bag was getting lighter! That story made Maria laugh. He was the only one that could do that.

Even though Maria and Hannah got along, they still argued a lot, usually about Nikolai. Hannah wouldn't like what he was doing, and Maria would defend him, and that would start an argument. Hannah didn't like him. It was her house, and we all lived with her, but Nikolai lived there without her approval.

Sometimes, Nikolai was nice to Hannah. When I was really little, they got along better. If Nikolai had a bottle, the two would get excited. They would start taking shots and be friendly with each other for the first 20 minutes. Then the friction started, and things rolled downhill as they started arguing, "Give me two more." "No." "What clsc are you going to do with it? Let's finish it." That's how it was between them all the time until the day everything changed forever.

There were only a couple of days of Paskha, the Easter holiday, left before Maria would take me back to the orphanage. Hannah and Maria started arguing over something about the house. Hannah said, "I'm leaving the house to Andry - not you!" Then Nikolai said something, and Maria got mad at him, too. The three were arguing all around me while I sat at the table eating. Maria said to Nikolai, "Why don't you tell your son how great you are." I quietly continued eating my lunch and wondered, "What's that about?" Nikolai didn't respond, so she continued. She was talking to me, but what she said was meant for him. "At the end of your last visit, there wasn't enough money for Nikolai and me to take you back to the orphanage, so I went, and Nikolai stayed home. He and Hannah got drunk, and he raped her." Hannah started crying and said to her, "Andry didn't need to know that."

For the first few days, I was really bothered. I couldn't talk to Nikolai. After that, I tried not to think about it. Any type of rape is wrong, no matter the reason. I can watch a scary movie, but if a movie has a rape scene, my blood goes up. Even though I know the scene is fake, it feels so real I can't watch it. It really bothers me. I don't like to be bothered for a long time, so the only thing I could do was forget about what Nikolai had done to Hannah. I couldn't do anything about it, anyway, but you never really forget, no matter how hard you try.

There is a saying in Ukraine. You can tell if a good man lives in a house because the house has a good gate. The house we lived in didn't have a gate at all.

Most of the gates in the village are painted with storks, flowers, or designs.
Green, blue, and purple are the most popular colors.

8. Olga

(Pippa's story)

She looked so small sitting on the chair, looking down and swinging her feet as she waited. She was wearing jeans and a faded red track jacket. A red plastic headband decorated her boy-short hair. While Irina and our driver, Tolya, stood in the hallway and talked to the orphanage director, we watched Olga through the doorway. We couldn't wait to meet her.

The others were still busy talking, so I went into the director's office and sat next to Olga. I showed her the Russian children's book we had gotten in the US, where you have to find the duck in each picture. We looked for the ducks together. She was quiet but engaged and adorable. Ron sat catty-corner from us. He and I caught eyes and smiled, thinking the same thing, "How could we NOT adopt her!"

Soon, the others came in and brought Olga's friend, Lisa, with them. Olga brightened and got more bubbly. She had acted reserved and kind of shy. Lisa was not shy. She was boisterous and quickly and loudly pointed to the duck in each picture, letting us know she had found the duck first before Olga. Then Ron realized that the girls were naming the items on the pages in Spanish. We understood what they were saying!

Through our interpreter, the orphanage staff explained that Olya and Lisa had been to "summer camp" in Spain. Both girls had only been at this orphanage since September. "Wait! What had they called her...Olya? What a beautiful name!" They explained that Olya, along with Olinka and Oleechka, were nicknames for Olga. But our Olga was known as Olya. Ron and I laughed at my relief.

They explained that through a program called Chernobyl Children, Spanish families sponsored Ukrainian orphans, allowing the children to get out of the contaminated region and get clean air, food, and water, reducing their risk of getting cancer. In 1988, the #4 reactor at the Chernobyl nuclear power plant had a meltdown that killed thousands and contaminated half of Ukraine and even surrounding countries. The orphanage was only 90 miles from the now-abandoned town of Chernobyl.

Olya had spent two summers and winter holidays with a host family in Spain. Her brother's host family had adopted him a year earlier. They had tried to adopt both of her brothers, but the older one had refused. If a child is over 10, they get to choose to go or not. We were told the family did not want a girl. We couldn't believe a judge had divided the children. We decided if we adopted her, we would get the info on the two boys so Olya could remain in contact with them.

Ron asked the director for permission to videotape the girls. They loved having their pictures taken, and Ron played the video back so they could see themselves. Through the interpreter, I asked the girls if they knew a song they could sing for us. I showed them they should stand next to each other. Lisa was much bolder and self-assured. She wiggled her hips and loved performing. Olya was cute as could be but more reserved. Then, the girls had to go back to class. We asked about the possibility of adopting both girls. We thought the director might have brought Lisa into the room for that reason, but no. They invited her so Olya would feel more comfortable. Smart of them. Olya was shy, and we wouldn't have seen her personality come out so quickly without a friend around. Lisa's parents visited, so she was not available to be adopted. There is no Ukrainian equivalent for the word orphanage. Instead, they have live-in schools called internats that act as orphanages and foster homes. Poor families can even leave their children at the internat until they are financially stable again.

We talked to the doctor, who said Olya was very healthy. She did have hernia surgery in 2000, but that was the only problem she had. Her teacher said she was a bright girl and had done well the month she'd been at school. She had no behavior problems and paid attention in class. She liked working on puzzles and drawing. She was careful. Then we went to see her music class.

On the way to the class, a group of about a dozen children crowded around me, hugging my legs and calling Mama Mama, which is also what they call their teachers, who are all female. Most of the children in the orphanage were not adoptable, but they were too young to understand. They wanted us to take them home with us.

Once inside the next classroom building, a little one bumped into me and wrapped both arms around me. The child was wearing a big coat and a white Pokemon knit hat. When the little face looked up, it was Olya smiling at me. Then she took my hand and Irina's and walked us to her classroom. She sat next to Lisa and carefully listened to the teacher. By contrast, Lisa interrupted the teacher. The teacher sat at the piano and asked Lisa and another boy, Vasiliy, whose only parent, his father, was in prison, so he wasn't eligible for adoption, to come up and sing. Irina said the song was about picking mushrooms with Grandmother. Then, the teacher asked Olya to come up and sing. Lisa rolled her eyes and pouted. She wanted to continue to be the center of attention. Having the other two children standing with her made Olya feel comfortable, and she sang a solo. Ron videotaped the little concert. She did well. Later, she joined us in the director's office.

Ron and I showed Olya the pictures we had brought from home. When she saw a picture of our dog, she repeated his name, "Smudge," her first American word. Her second was "duck" because we kept looking for the hidden ducks in the picture book we had brought for her. Her third word was "Pippa," my name.

Olya, about a minute after we met her.

Lisa, Ron, and Olya, in the director's office, playing back the videos he had taken of the girls singing a song and doing a little dance together.

Several times a year, the children in the orphanage put on elaborate pageants with costumes, dancing, songs, and skits. They spent weeks rehearsing. In this photo, Olya is second from the right.

9. Freedom

(Andry's story)

One winter night, Maria went to work. She locked the three of us in the house so we wouldn't walk around outside without jackets on. We were just little kids and could walk far and freeze to death. She thought we would be safe if we stayed in the house with Hannah, our grandmother, who was sleeping.

I found the key on top of the green door, which is the entrance to the house. I unlocked the door and put the key back on the other side. I could do that because, above the door, there is a hole through the wall. I didn't want to take my little sister and brother, Olya and Dima, with me because I wanted to follow Maria to see where she would go.

She saw me and said to go back to the house. I pretended to go back but instead kept following her from a distance. She went to the collective farm where she worked. I think she got milk and went back home.

When we were near the farm, I lost her. It was very cold outside. Everything was white. It was like the time Dima and I made a house out of snow. It was so big it had rooms that we could stand up inside. We weren't very tall, though.

At the farm, I had my favorite cow. She was orange. One time, I wanted to take her home, but she was not a puppy that I could hide easily. That night, I stayed petting the orange cow, taking food from other cows to give her. I really liked her, but she didn't give a lot of milk. If a cow didn't give milk, she would be killed for meat. She had the red mark on her forehead that meant she was to be killed. I spit on my hand to try to take the paint off her head.

It was nighttime, around 10:00. My house was far away, and I was small and tired, and I wanted to go to sleep. Inside the house for cows, it was cold, but not as cold as it was outside. The building was long, with cows on each side, and the soloma and hay to feed them were piled in the middle. I was wearing a little *kurtochka* (which means jacket in Ukrainian). It was big for me because Maria didn't have much money to buy us clothes in our sizes. I wore it, then Dima, then Olya. That night, I slept in the hay. It was very hot in there, and I had to take the kurtochka off. Inside the hay, I would breathe, and everything around me would get too warm. Then, I had to crawl to a colder place in the hay.

In the morning, when I woke up, it was bright outside the windows and very freezing, but where I was sleeping was hot. I got up and thought, "Where am I?" Then I realized where I was.

I was old enough to walk in the village. I never told Maria where I was going, but she always knew. If I was missing, I was at the collective farm. It was an interesting place to wander around.

You could do a lot of stuff when no one was watching you. It's like freedom. When I was small, I had the most freedom I've ever had. In the village, nothing bad could happen to you. I wasn't afraid to walk by myself. Everyone knew me. Why would anyone want to bother me?

One time, there was a drunk guy I knew, but I didn't know him well. He started pushing and insulting me, and he hit me in the face across my cheek. I hadn't done anything; I was just walking by myself. When Nikolai, my biological father, got drunk, he went and beat the man because he had hit me. Nikolai also beat Maria one night because she wouldn't go buy him more vodka. That's what alcohol does to innocent people.

On the way back to my house from the cows, lived a woman who would always invite me in for *varenya* (means jam in Ukrainian). When

I was walking to her house, I was excited because that was where I would get my breakfast. She told me I didn't have to knock because she might not hear me. "Just go in," she always said. She usually had breakfast ready for me because I always came around 7:00. I got up early.

One morning, I came into the kitchen, and she wasn't there. I went to her bedroom, where there was a long, round piece of wood that ran down the middle of the ceiling. It had a hook with a rope. She was hanging, and the chair had fallen.

She was tall with red hair and some golden teeth. She always wore a *hustka* (which means scarf in Ukrainian). Now, I guess she was 60-70, but then I didn't even know how old my own grandmother was.

I went home. Instead of telling Maria, I asked her, "You want to visit the woman with the red hair and tell her hi?" Maria found her and called the neighbors. The next time I saw the woman, she was in a coffin being carried by six men from the village. I walked next to the men. I never understood why she hung herself. We were friends.

When my mom, sister, and I went back to Ukraine for a visit, we asked around the village if anyone knew why the redheaded woman had taken her life. We found out the woman's husband had died the year before. She had not been able to handle the loneliness. Now, they are next to each other in the cemetery.

10. Hello Spain

(Andry's story)

Roma waved at people he knew, so I waved at them, too, and they waved back at me. He got picked up, but I was still waiting. There were about 30 chairs, and when I looked around, besides me, there were only 3-4 kids left. Everyone else had gone with host parents. I started getting nervous. There were still a lot of people in the room, but I sat alone by myself. Finally, the organizing man called my name, and I walked to him like the other kids had done. A man walked up to me and started hugging me. I stood straight with my hands at my side, thinking, "He's friendly."

He held my hand, and we walked out. He gave me the sign asking if I had to go to the bathroom. I didn't have to, but he did. I waited until he came out. I sat in the back seat of the car, playing with a toy action figure I had found in the middle console. Emilio, the man, drove to his apartment in Cordoba. He unlocked the door, and we walked up the spiral stairs, then down a long hall and into an apartment. I remember a table filled with candies, chocolates, and ice cream. A woman my size was waiting for us. She asked if I wanted anything. I wasn't hungry, so I just sat.

They handed me something shaped like a Snickers bar. I said, "I'm not hungry," but I knew they didn't understand what I had said. Emilio opened the wrapper, and I was surprised because inside was a watch, a Mickey Mouse watch. I was so tired. I put my hands together and held them next to my cheek. They nodded "yes" and took me back down the hall to a big bed with huge pillows and a puffy comforter. A few hours later, I woke up and went to the bathroom. A girl, Jessy, was brushing her teeth and talking to me in Spanish.

A few months later, when I flew back to Ukraine from Spain and went back to Pirioslove, my second orphanage, I had forgotten every single word of Ukrainian. I could only find Spanish words. It was as if I had never known Ukrainian.

I was with Roma playing on the floor in the room I shared with him and the 16 other boys in my grade. I told him that I was thirsty. He said I should ask the teacher, who was watching us, for water. When I told her, "Yo tengo sed." she just looked at me and then went back to what she was doing. I went back to Roma and told him that she wouldn't answer me. When he translated for me, the teacher started laughing. It was so crazy. How could I have forgotten my language?

In this photo I am seven, and at the beach in Fuengirola, Spain, where my host family had a vacation condo. I stayed with them every summer and winter holiday until I was 13.

My best friend, Roma, is on the far left, and I'm in the middle. When I was 16, my mom took me back to Ukraine for visit, which included seeing my orphanage friends in Bucha.

11. Playdate

(Pippa's story)

We went to play with Olya, but soon her entire class was in the room with us. The other children acted much freer with us investigating everything about our clothes, hair, fingers, and my purse. I took my lipstick out and showed the girls, all crowded around me, how they could apply pink on their lips and then make kisses on paper. One of the little boys wanted to try, too. A little odd but fine with me. Three hours later, I found out he was she. The orphanage had cut her hair so short.

I wanted special playtime with Olya, but it was impossible because all 17 kids wanted attention. Lisa would get upset when I moved the focus from her to include Olya or the other children. She would retaliate by pulling my shirt up to expose me. That only had to happen once! When her exposing technique didn't work anymore, she moved on to trying to unbuckle my pants.

Some of the boys were fooling around with a little pink purse. I noticed that the purse had a crayon word written on it: Natasha. Olya also saw the action and marched over and resolutely wrestled the little purse away from the boys. Then she left the room. I knew she was on a mission to find Natasha, her classmate, and return her purse.

The children seemed to have been left alone in our care. Ron and I had run out of indoor activities, so we took the group outside to find the playground. Ron videotaped our parade, turning the viewfinder backward so the kids could see themselves. They mugged for the camera, making all sorts of faces. At the playground, we discovered the swingset had no swings, the slide had no ladder, and the monkey bars had no bars. Everything was in such disrepair. We needed a new plan.

The older kids that were hanging around got curious and came over fascinated by the video camera fun. We asked them their names, "Yak tebe zvati" and recorded their answers. The playback got giggles from them all. The activities director, Nadia, showed up. She helped me organize the 25 kids, ages 6-15, in a spontaneous game. I would demonstrate some sort of action like a spin or jumping jack, then count "1, 2, 3," and all the kids would do the same action in unison with me.

The kindergarten teacher finally showed up, but only to get Olya because her "Spanish Mama" was on the phone. Alarmed, Ron and I looked at each other, "What's going on!" Tolla quickly followed Olya to investigate. He later told us Olya went to the phone, picked up the receiver, and put it down without ever speaking into the handset.

I'm playing Simon Says with the kids.

12. Forever

(Andry's story)

The three of us were in different orphanages. I lived the farthest away. Maria would come from the village to pick me up, and on the way back, we would get Dima or Olya. I don't remember her ever picking up all three of us. After we were put in the orphanage, I have no memory of all three of us ever being together.

As usual, she picked me up to take me back to the village to spend the holiday. On the way back to the village, we stopped to get Dima, the second oldest. He was in a different orphanage. When we got to his school and checked in with his teacher, she told us he was in the hospital. Something was wrong with his appendix.

All of the orphanages I ever saw, the orphanages I was in, and the ones my brother and sister lived in were surrounded by fruit trees. During recess, the kids would go out to play and sneak off to the trees to eat the fruit. I loved eating apricots. It didn't matter if they were ripe. The teachers tell kids that if you eat fruit that isn't ready to be eaten, it hurts your appendix. So when we were told Dima was in the hospital, it made sense to me that something was wrong with his appendix. I didn't know where the appendix was, but I imagined it was on the side of your stomach, and you would get a bubble there if you ate too much green fruit.

Maria and I left Dima's orphanage and took two different buses to get to the hospital. She didn't have much money, so this was expensive for her.

Once there, we asked to see Dima Burlaka. The hospital carefully went through the records, and even the doctors said he wasn't there. Maria and I went back to the orphanage and asked them again, "Where is Dima?" That's when the orphanage told us he had been adopted.

Maria was furious that she hadn't been told and that the orphanage had lied to her. The orphanage had us pointlessly search for him and worry about him being ill. She was especially upset because there were two laws that weren't being followed. One law says when your kid goes to the orphanage, you have the right to see them and pick them up as you please for visits. It's as if your kid is just at boarding school. Another law says if you are having regular contact with your child, you have to be notified when your child is adopted. Since she was regularly visiting us, she had the right to be notified.

I was confused because I didn't know what "adopted" meant. I just knew Dima had left, and he wasn't coming back to the village with us. I didn't understand that I would never see him again. Maria tried to explain the reality to me, but I didn't understand the concept of forever. Back then, I couldn't imagine life more than a few days ahead.

This photo of Maria holding me is the earlisdt photo I hae of myself.

13. My Birthday Party

(Pippa's story)

Tolya got back in the car and let us know that we would go to court the next morning and get to take Olya after that. No waiting. Usually, there was a two-week waiting period. A few minutes before, he and a woman from one of the buildings, city hall or the courthouse, had walked across the parking lot, stopped and spoke in an animated way, and then walked around the back of the building. They stayed around the corner for just a couple of minutes. Is that how bribes are given? Who cares! Ron and I couldn't wait for our family to be 3 ½. Ron pointed out that Smudge, our dog, should not be counted as the 1/2 since he was certainly bigger than Olya.

Coincidentally, this day was my birthday. To celebrate, we took cake, ice cream, and a present for each of the 17 children in Olya's class. The present was a pencil case with colored pencils, paper, markers, a ruler, and a magnifying glass. When we arrived, our two favorite staffers had presents for me! How had they known it was my birthday? When you know Ukrainians, they are so big-hearted. I appreciated the chocolate, flowers, and champagne, but they should have spent every penny on the kids—maybe on the playground toilet. The worst gas station bathroom in the United States is better than what the children had to use. When Mother Nature called very loudly, I had to use the toilet at the playground, which is a small outbuilding with a tiled hole in the floor. I nearly vomited. The stench was unbearable, and it was winter. I can't imagine how ripe the place was in August. Fortunately, the indoor bathroom was more civilized but was missing the doors on its toilet stalls.

Olya sat at the front of the class with me. She carefully selected just the right case (they had different pictures on them) for each child. Olya liked being in charge, and the children loved their gifts.

Olya playing with her best friends at the orphanage, Lisa and Vasily.

14. Control

(Andry's story)

The cops I knew had a decent house and were somehow good. They didn't drink as much. They were aware of right and wrong. They knew you couldn't hit your wife. They didn't have as much violence in their families.

There was one that constantly came for Nikolai. He was friendly and nice to me, a big guy with a big belly. He told me I should try to control Nikolai because he wasn't doing anything good. It didn't take me long to realize I did have control over him. I could manipulate Nikolai when he was drunk. I could say, "Let's not do that. Let's do this instead." I knew there was something in me that could tell Nikolai not to do something. That's a good skill to have.

I was with Maria, walking back from the grocery store when we saw Nikolai. He was going to see his dad and told me to go with him. I told Maria I didn't want to go. He said, "Come, you'll have fun." I knew everyone would just get drunk, and I wouldn't have anything to do and be bored. The only reason I didn't mind going there occasionally was because Didusha, Nikolai's father, would give me money.

When Nikolai came back from his father's house, I knew he was upset with me. He was ignoring me, then told me, "You're a mommy's boy." I knew I needed to make up a good story about why I didn't go with him, or he was going to get really mad.

Every village has someone in charge. The guy who asked me about my hat was in charge of our village. I told Nikolai that I hadn't gone with him because that man wanted to see me about my school. I knew I had to bullshit something important, something official, so he wouldn't be mad. Nikolai said, "Oh, okay."

15. Best Present Ever

(Pippa's story)

The courthouse steps were crumbling with exposed rebar ready to jab you in the ankle if you didn't step carefully enough. In the States, it would be "a lawsuit waiting to happen." Inside was dark, lit only by the light from the windows, and cold. Either it wasn't yet the official day when the country turned on the heat, or there just wasn't any heat in the building. The children's bedrooms at the orphanage weren't heated, so in an attempt to reassure us, we were told each child had TWO blankets. I wished I had two blankets right then; I was shaking from the cold and excitement.

Ron, Olya, two really warm and wonderful administrators from her orphanage and I waited for our turn to go before the judge and officially make Olya our daughter (or so we hoped.) Finally, we all went into his small rectangular-shaped chambers, still dressed in our coats, hats, and gloves, and sat on two long benches that lined each side. His desk was in the middle at one end.

He acknowledged us but wasn't friendly and didn't make eye contact. Speaking rapidly and efficiently he rattled in Ukrainian to Nadia and Svetlana. We had no idea what he was saying. The ladies looked tense as he flipped through our dossier, carefully examining the information and asking them lots of questions. Ron and I nervously cut our eyes at each other. Did he like us? Did he think we were good parents for Olya?

After forever, he looked up at us and smiled. He had five gold teeth and the bluest eyes I had ever seen. "So, you have horses. Me too," he said in perfect English. He went on and said to me, "Today I am giving you the best birthday present ever, a little girl who looks just like you!" My eyes welled up with tears, and my heart sang at full blast.

Olya and me in 2002, drawing together in the orphanage classroom.

Olya and me in 2014. People were always surprised when they found out Olya was adopted because they thought she looked like me.

16. First Things

(Andry's story)

I think I remember coming out of a vagina. Inside, everything was orange, and I was floating toward a pink thing like a jellyfish. Then I was dragged out, and it was very bright. The next thing I remember is being next to Maria on the bed in the hospital. It felt like birth, but you can't remember your own birth. It had to be a dream. If it was a dream, that dream is one of the first things I remember.

I remember when Dima, my younger brother, was born. Nikolai, my father, and I went to the hospital to see Maria. I was wandering by myself around the hospital. It was so big. Down a hall to the left, I saw a long table of people in white eating, and I walked up to them. A doctor picked me up and started talking to me. I don't know, but I assume he was asking me if I was lost.

When Olya, my sister, was born, Nikolai and I went to the hospital again, but they wouldn't let us inside. We had to stay outside in the cold. It was December 25th. There was snow on the ground. There was a playground next to the hospital and a place to sit. Then Maria came to the door and leaned out to talk to us. It was too cold for her to come out. We went to the steps by the door. She asked what I had been doing with Nikolai. Then Nikolai and I went home. On the walk back to the village, we saw a giant crane's nest on the top of a power pole. I wanted to climb up. Was it warm in the nest? What did it look like from way up there?

Crane nests are common in the village. When I was 18 I designed a tattoo of a crane and have it over my heart.

17. The Sidecar

(Andry's story)

When Nikolai came home, he was on an old-school motorcycle with a sidecar. Nikolai said that someone had given it to him but Maria didn't believe him. She said, "Why would someone give it to you? Why would they do that!" It would have been more believable if he had said that he bought it because no one would give him anything like that. It was in great shape. I really liked the wheels.

He took me for a long ride. We went past where the hay was stored on the edge of the village to where one of his friends lived in the mountains in Vinnetsya. It was cold and windy sitting in the sidecar. I was sitting on my knees. Around the seat was a cloth that covered my body so that only my head showed. We were driving through the typical Ukrainian landscape of wheat fields with small, long lines of dark trees. Just my eyes were peeking up over the side of the car.

His friend's house was baby blue on the bottom and white on top and had a barn. There was a field of crops going down the hill and a stream at the bottom. The guy had a lot of fishing gear I had never seen before. I wanted to steal it so I could learn how to fish with the big nets.

To go home, Nikolai drove a wagon pulled by two horses. There was a very steep hill, so steep I thought I would roll out of the back of the wagon. I laid flat.

I remember being at the man's house once before with everyone for a holiday. Nikolai kept sending me to go get more beer. I remember thinking, "Why doesn't Olya do it?" Olya was super small. Maria was carrying her on her hip. She could walk, though, so she could have done it.

When Olya and I went back to Ukraine with my mom when we were 16 and 13, we visited the village. I helped Olya ask Maria if she had any baby photos of her. This is the earliest photo of Olya that exists.

18. Circus Tickets

(Pippa's story)

When you adopt a child, you just get the child, not the clothes they are wearing. You must bring clothes for them to change into; the clothes the child is wearing belong to the orphanage.

Once a week, Olya's teacher would bring out a big, black garbage bag of clothes for the children in the class to look through and pick out what they wanted to wear. Valari, one of the boys in her class, had been wearing a girl's sweater with a cute bear on the front when we met him.

Each grade of children was a unit and lived on a schedule. Together, they woke up, ate, went to school, played, showered, and went to bed at the same time. Selecting what to wear was one of the only things that the children decided on their own. It was a way for them to express their individuality.

Since we were prevented from taking Olya for several days, even after she had legally become our daughter, Ron and I had plenty of time to shop for her clothes. We looked in the Ukrainian department stores, but the little girl's clothes were so incredibly ugly. We couldn't bear to see our cute little thing dressed so hideously. We gave up and just bought panties and tights that would be hidden under her other clothes anyway.

Against the advice of our frugal Ukrainian translator, we went to Benetton, where the clothes were quite expensive, much more expensive than the same clothes would have been in the States. We bought Olya lots of pink. My favorite was a hot pink coat with fake fur around the cuffs, which was adorable, along with a light pink hat and, matching scarf and gloves. At a fluffy French store called Elephant, we found shiny maroon shoes with navy trim.

On our third trip to the orphanage to pick her up, they said we could take her with us. Finally, she was ours! We had the three outfits we had gotten for Olya and let her pick which she wanted to wear. She picked the jeans and a pink, teal, and tan striped sweater. She stripped off her ill-fitting orphanage clothes. On her bottom and down the back of her right leg was a scar caused by a burn. I winced, thinking how painful that had been for her. How did it happen? Was it an accident or punishment? A friend had adopted a little boy from Bulgaria. The boy's biological father sat him on the stove because the boy had lost a shoe. We hoped Olya's scar was from an accident. There was so much we didn't know about her.

Olya bounced in her new clothes. She was so excited, but instead of putting on her new pink hat, she insisted on wearing her dingy, worn Pokemon hat. Olya told the translator something; her brother had given her the hat. It was special to her, but she wasn't allowed to take it because the hat was officially the property of the orphanage. We happily offered the pink Benetton hat as a trade.

She also had with her a plastic FedEx bag that contained all her possessions: a Tweety Bird necklace, a half-eaten bag of sunflower seeds, and a piece of bubble wrap. The address on the bag was from Spain.

Before we left, the orphanage staff told us a few final things about Olya. Her biological parents had visited her sometimes. Her oldest brother was still in a Ukrainian orphanage, but they didn't know where. Her foster family from Spain had visited intending to adopt her but left for some unknown reason. Her middle brother had been adopted by a family in Spain. They supplied us with the family's name and the city where they lived. Their information didn't match the name on the FedEx bag.

Just before we all got in the car, the school administrators carefully explained something to Olya in Ukrainian. When we were in the privacy of the car, I asked Irina what they had said. Fearing Olya would resist leaving the orphanage, the administrators told her, "These people are taking you to the circus." We couldn't start our relationship with her with a lie! Ron and I hoped there was a circus in town. As luck had it, there was. We bought tickets and went that night.

The day before we met Olya, they had cut all the girls' hair for wintertime. Short hair dried faster than long hair and kept the girls warmer in the cold weather. Olya missed her long hair. At the circus, they sold colorful, shiny foil wigs. She had long hair again.

Olya wearing her colorful, foil wig and playing in our very cold apartment In Kiev.

19. The Red Cabinet

(Andry's story)

There was a certain kind of gum. Each piece came wrapped in paper with a different picture: motorcycles, naked girls, cartoons... anything. Maria would paste the papers to the outside of the red cabinet where she kept medicine. I was fascinated with syringes. She had some in the red cabinet. Maria never did any kind of drug. I never even saw her take a shot. In the village, it was typical for people to have basic medicines since most didn't have a car to get to a doctor.

I should probably be dead now or have some ugly disease. On the way to the lake, there was a big hole where the people in the village would dump their trash. That place was paradise for me. I would find syringes with stuff in them. I had it in my mind to poke it in me, but I knew it wasn't healthy.

I did use them for one good purpose. I didn't know how to cook, but I would mix dirt, leaves, and water. Then, take the syringe, pull up some of the mixture, put it somewhere else, let the mixture dry, and turn it over. When it dried, there were really cool sculptures. Sometimes, I used fire to make the sculptures harden faster. I would build a fire behind the outhouse.

I remember a lot of things about fire. People now would say, "Are you crazy!" But I never hurt anything. Sometimes, I would build huge fires. I would steal gasoline from Nikolai's friend, put it in a little cup, put my hand over it, run home, and put it on a fire I had started. He didn't live close, so it was a lot of work to accomplish nothing, well, except burn the front of my hair.

I remember I was by myself most of the time. Only one time, when a lot of flowers came up in the forest, Maria, Hannah, Olya, and I went to pick the flowers.

Our village was pretty small. Walking around didn't take long. Going to the grocery would take 10 minutes there and 10 back unless you stopped to talk to people. I always liked to be going to see something. It was interesting to know everything and see everything. But when I was little, the village was big. Now it's small because I see it as streets. Back then, it was a series of places.

Outside the village, in the summertime, there were huge piles of hay, bigger than a bus. Inside the hay were chicken eggs, and we would throw them on the ground.

I don't remember who I was with or if I was alone, but I would leave the village and go to a place where there were fields of wheat. Back then, there were hay stacks that were super tall, five times taller than I am, two stories tall, and five stories long. They fascinated me. I wondered what was on top. I dug a hole in the side and then a spiral tunnel to the top of the stack. I sat on top, with my feet hanging over, and saw everything. I slept there.

I was walking around on top, exploring what different views looked like. I also found bird nests with eggs and left them. The next time I came, there were baby birds.

There used to be a garden in the front of the house. Nikolai would make a hole; I would put in two potato pieces; Maria would pour the water; then Nikolai would close the hole. When Hannah could walk and knew where she was, she helped in the garden. Hannah would plant the potatoes at home, and we would do it for other people to make money. Then she got old, and we planted the potatoes at home, too.

The red cabinet covered with the stickers that come in gum packets.

20. Nikolai Never Did

(Andry's story)

Maria was making an outside cooking house with three walls and a roof. She was up on the roof and sent me to get Nikolai to help. I didn't know where he was so she told me to go look at his friend's house. I did, but Nikolai wasn't there. The friend said Nikolai left a while ago, and he was drunk. That meant he could be far away. As I was walking back to tell Maria, I heard something, some weird noises. I looked up to the point of the roof where the noise had come from.

In the triangular attic of the house, there was no wall. You could see inside. There was a lot of hay. I went up there because I thought Nikolai might have made the noise. He was really messed up. I told him he needed to come help, and he said he would. I really thought he would come, but he never did.

One of Nikolai's hiding places.

21. I Am Grateful to Scooby-Doo

(Pippa's story)

Our first night back in our own house felt so good. What we had thought would be a two-week trip to Ukraine to adopt a little girl had turned into five cold, frustrating weeks. While Ron and I were exhausted physically and mentally. Olya wasn't.

The first morning, she woke me up at 4:00 with "Piscina?" which I knew meant pool in Spanish. She was already dressed in her new bathing suit with the pink and green Hawaiian print flowers on it. Outside, it was still black. Somehow, I explained that we had to wait for the sun to come up before we could go to the public pool down the street.

While we waited, we watercolored. She painted the first of many brightly colored buildings with a cross on top. I wondered why this church had such a big influence on her. Was it the church down the street from her orphanage or a different one? Had she been to this church in Spain or maybe her village? Almost everything about her was a mystery and would be a mystery until she learned enough English to tell us her stories.

No matter how hard you try, you can't watercolor for five hours with a six-year-old. Fortunately, Cartoon Network was having a 24-hour Scooby-Doo marathon, my favorite cartoon as a child and one she had loved in Ukraine. We curled up in bed to watch until the sun, and I woke up.

Olya was always ready for the pool or the beach. This photo was taken when Olya had been in the U.S. for about a year. She was modeling for one our student's photo shoots.

22. Afraid

(Andry's story)

The first excuse Maria gave me was she fell. Then, when she and Hannah were arguing, Hannah told her, "Look what he did to your face. Leave him. Look what he's doing to you!" Maria stayed with him because she was afraid. Many times, he told her, "If you divorce me, I will kill you. I will set the house on fire."

Maria, Nikolai, and I were coming from the orphanage and were almost at the village. We had paid for a bus to get from Kiev to Titiev but, after that, we always had to walk the two hours to the village if it was late or there wasn't a bus. This time, someone gave us a ride from Titiev halfway to the village. While we were walking, Nikolai asked me, "What are you going to do when you grow up?" "Why don't you escape the orphanage and live with us?" "Maria and I will have another kid, and we will start things all over again." I agreed but knew none of that was going to happen. You don't start over. It's not possible.

I was in 5th grade. Fifth grade in the U.S. is very low, but in the village, it's much different. Since most people only go to 9th grade, as a 5th grader, you're more than halfway through school. You're not a child anymore.

I was thinking about what I would do when I was older, and I wanted to be a policeman. It's a job that doesn't require a lot of work, and you get your own car. I told Nikolai I wanted to be a cop. He laughed at me and said, "That isn't smart because you will be going after me." I knew he wouldn't like my answer, but I didn't expect him to say that! I said, "Just don't do things like steal and be mean, and I won't have to go after you."

23. Scribble-Dibble

(Pippa's story)

Before we left for Ukraine, I wrote all the important information, phone numbers, and instructions in a journal to take with us. I especially liked this book because each section had different colored paper. It was a happy book. I carried the book with us everywhere we went in Ukraine. When we had downtime, I would write about what was happening and the things we were feeling.

When we were with Olya and the other children, the journal became another way to play with them. I would trace my hand and then turn each fingertip into an animal by adding ears, a trunk, or whiskers. Then, Olya would trace her hand and make her own animals. Ron entertained her entire class with a page from the book and a pen. Surrounded by a crowd of six-year-olds, he would start drawing a cartoon complete with snarling, barking, or grunting sound effects. The kids would squeal with laughter as his lines turned into a dragon, cheetah, or dog. Then, he would draw silly cartoons of different kids. They would carefully watch until they recognized which kid he was drawing, and then that one would blush and giggle from the extra attention.

Sometimes, Olya would take the book and pen from me and fill pages and pages with scribbles. Then she would show it to us, and we would pretend to read what she had written, nodding and saying, "Ah, yes," as if it made sense to us.

One night, a few weeks after we had brought her home to Miami, I was tucking her into bed when Olya jumped up and ran downstairs. I had no idea why. Was she refusing to go to bed? We had found out she was a trickster. Was this some sort of last-minute game to delay bedtime? I knew it was important to have a routine because consistency gives kids security. What was I supposed to do? She had seemed so purpose-filled when she ran out the door. I decided to wait to see what her plan was.

In a few minutes, she ran back into her bedroom carrying a pad of paper and a pen. She handed them to me and pantomimed that I was supposed to write down what she said. She stood in front of me in the dimly lit room, explaining her story through a mixture of hand motions and a few English and Spanish words. Ever so often, she would point at the paper, which I knew meant to read back to her what I had written. When I hadn't gotten the story right, she would get exasperated, stamp her foot, and tell me, "No." Then, she would retell her story until I got my facts straight.

She was putting so much effort into explaining her story, and I was trying hard to figure out what she was telling me. This was the first time she had shared anything about her past. I knew this story was important to her. At the same time, I laughed inside at how impossible my task was. How in the world was I to understand her complicated stories from so little information?

In one story, she grabbed the front of her shirt, pretended to throw it down, and said, agua, Spanish for water. Then she held up both fists in the air and extended her arms, pantomiming punching. What in the world did that mean?! Who was punching? Was someone being punched? Was agua a wash tub, a lake, rain...?

I knew her biological parents' names, so I asked if the person doing the punching was Nikolai, and she nodded, "Yes." My heart sank. I calmly asked if Nikolai was punching her. She shook her head, "No." What a relief it was to hear she hadn't been hit. Understanding Olya's story was a process of elimination. Was Nikolai punching Maria? Olya nodded, "Yes." I wondered if the burn on her bottom and back of her leg was an accident or a punishment he had given her. I asked about the agua but couldn't find a way of determining if Maria had not washed Nikolai's shirt, so he had punched her, and so she started cleaning it as he had wanted. Or maybe he had punched her, and she said, "Screw you, buddy, and tossed his shirt in the river." I hoped it was the latter.

To try to understand better, I asked Olya, "What did you do?" She took her finger and ran it down her cheek. She had cried.

To entertain Olya, I traced my hand and turned my fingertips into animals.

When I gave Olya my journal, she created her own hand drawing.

24. Apples and Oranges

(Andry's story)

It was a regular day of second grade at the Pereyaslav Khmelnytsky orphanage. My teacher came to me and said, "Your brother is here." I knew she was wrong. Then, in the distance, I saw my brother sitting in a car with some people. They looked like parents. They spoke Spanish, and since I had spent two summer and winter holidays with a host family in Spain, I knew a lot of Spanish. We could talk. They invited me to go eat with them at a restaurant, a pretty good one. On the outside was a blue tent with writing on it that said Obolon, a type of beer. We walked through the tent and sat down at a table inside the restaurant.

The parents ordered something to eat but didn't talk that much to me. They were pale and acted grey. That made me feel like they would be very strict. They did explain, "We are Dima's parents, and we are here to visit you." I didn't want to talk to them. I was a little mad because they had taken Dima, and I knew how that had hurt Maria. Plus, they were strangers to me, and I'm not comfortable around strangers.

The whole time we were at the restaurant, I talked to Dima in Ukrainian. Dima told me, "You can come to Spain and live with me. We live in an apartment." I wondered how many bedrooms were in the apartment. I thought as Dima and I grew up, we wouldn't be fond of each other and wouldn't want to share a bedroom. He said, "For now, just one." After we ate, Dima and I went to a glass case where candy was for sale. I was staring at a pack of Orbit gum, but it was quite expensive. I asked Dima if he could get me the gum. He said, "Yes."

The mother was more of the leader. She paid the bill. If the father is weak and doesn't take charge, there isn't stability in a family, so the mother HAS to lead. That's the way it seemed with Dima's parents. Two weak parents and a brother I knew I would be fighting with. After all, we are both boys. Of course, his mother would side with him because he is younger, and that's always the case. I knew they had money. I even asked if they would help Maria, but I felt like I would be left out and unhappy. That's the feeling I had when I hung out with them that day.

After lunch, they dropped me off at the orphanage, and I said, "I'll think about it and let you know what I decide." They told me to let them know soon because they were only in Ukraine for a couple of more days. It was right before Saint Andry's Day, November 30th, my birthday. I was going to be ten. It was also time for our autumn break from school.

The next day Maria came to pick me up for the holiday. I told her about the day before with Dima and his parents. She asked, "You're not going to go, are you?!" I told her no. I didn't want to disappoint her or even Nikolai. Since Dima and Olya were already adopted, I was the only child left.

Then Maria and I took the bus to Kiev to spend the night at my great aunt Hallah's apartment. When Maria came from the village to get me, we would always spend the night in the city visiting Hallah, her grown son, daughter, and their spouses before taking the next morning's bus to the village. The apartment had two bedrooms where the couples slept. Hallah and her grandson shared the living room, but he would sleep with his parents when Maria and I visited. We slept on the pull-out sofa.

I remember being on the balcony of the apartment. I knew Dima's parents were coming back to the orphanage the next day, and I wouldn't be there. I looked down at the street and school below, watching the passing buses, wondering if I had made the right choice.

This photo was taken at my first-grade graduation. Six months later, Dima, Olya, and I were taken to the orphanage.

25. At First There Was The Collective Farm

(Andry's story)

Almost everyone in the village worked on the kolhosp, the collective farm, doing something. Maria was working in a long building, milking cows. There were cows and horses. Maria worked with the cows. Nikolai worked with the horses. When Maria did fun things, I stayed with her. When Nikolai rode horses, I went with him.

There were 100 cows. Maria took care of one line of cows. Another woman took care of another line. Her son came many times to help her. He had a small-sized pitchfork. I became friends with him, and I asked if I could have it. I wanted to put the hay for the cows to eat with the pitchfork. The boy said "no," so, eventually, I took it.

His family had animals and pigs. I went past their house at night to their shed, took the pitchfork, and ran back to my house. I had it for a couple of days. Nikolai asked where I got the pitchfork, so I told him, "I found it."

I was with Nikolai taking down the hay, and the woman saw me with the pitchfork and said I stole it. I said that I didn't steal it and that the pitchfork was mine. If I told the truth, Nikolai would find out I lied to him. When Nikolai left, Maria told me to give the pitchfork back to the woman because it wasn't mine. Maria and the woman worked next to each other.

The farm was a huge place with a lot of horses. There were more cows than horses, but they had at least 40 horses. I always wanted to have a favorite horse. In the middle stable, they had a huge, black, hairy horse. I could easily walk under him without ducking, but I was too scared to go in the stall. I was almost too scared to look at him because when I looked at him, he would snort. One of the men who worked on the farm tried to ride him and got killed. He thought he was brave, showing off. After that, they sold the horse.

Nikolai's work was to get horses and take them to the field where there was a lot of hay. He would load the hay on the wagon and take it to the barns until they were all filled. It would take a couple of hours. They had to do it in the ranok, dehn, and vechir. Morning, midday, and night.

In between these times, Nikolai taught me to ride, but not on the back of the horses, behind two horses on a wagon. He would get different horses from the ones he worked with, good ones, easier to ride. We would go to the fields for my lesson. The horses know trrrr (stop) or ch, ch (go). I learned how to make the horses go back, turn to the left, and sometimes run. Nikolai would make them run fast as hell, and I would be sitting next to him, holding on.

The village's source of income, the collective farm, closed a few years after the Soviet Union fell in 1991. When this photo was taken, the once bustling cow barn had been standing empty for a decade.

In the village, it is still common to use a horse and wagon for work and transportation.

26. Pink Dog

(Pippa's story)

Olya and I were baking Christmas cookies. I had gotten all sorts of sprinkles and icing, and we were having fun decorating together and admiring each other's cookie masterpieces. She had been home with us for two months, and I was always looking for ways to interact with her that didn't require language. She understood a lot of English but could only speak a few words.

"Mama," the way she said it always made me feel like I was in a French film, "Olya Pink Dog." She hadn't yet learned "I" or "me" and referred to herself in the third person. I thought pretending she was a dog could be a fun game. Our big, brown lab, the most cuddly, kissable dog ever, had been hanging around, hoping we would drop something tasty on the floor. I took Smudge's collar off over his head and put it on Olya, who was on her hands and knees on the kitchen floor. I put down two bowls of water and started breaking up the cookies and tossing them for Olya and Smudge to catch. Smudge was happy that Olya missed most of hers. All three of us were laughing.

As if carefully taking the next step, Olya said, "Mama, Olya, baby Pink Dog." I felt like my college psych professor had reached up out of the textbook and slapped me in the face. I knew what Olya was doing and what she was really saying! You treat a puppy very differently than you do a grown dog. Olya was telling me she wanted affection. She was affectionate with strangers and would even sit on their laps and take their hands, but

64

she wasn't affectionate with Ron and me. If I tried to hug her or kiss her forehead goodnight, she would sternly tell me, "Malo," which means "bad" in Spanish.

I sat down, patted my lap, and said, "Does Pink Dog want to sit on my lap?" She nodded and crawled as a dog would onto my lap. I hugged and rocked her and kissed the top of her head, and she loved it. She didn't pull away or tell me, "Malo." Finally, the affection I had been wanting to give and receive.

When children don't feel safe, they pretend to be someone else. By inventing Pink Dog, Olya was testing to see if it was safe to love and be loved. If Pink Dog was rejected, it wouldn't be a rejection of her. After that, Pink Dog showed up a lot, but only around me, not around Ron. Neither of us could touch Olya affectionately, but I could snuggle Pink Dog.

One Sunday afternoon, about a month later, Ron went to play soccer, so Olya and I were home alone. I had a feeling Pink Dog would appear. I loved Pink Dog and knew how important Pink Dog time was for Olya, but after the third hour, it got tiring. You see, playing with a dog for hours is easy. Playing with a little girl for hours is easy. Playing with a little girl pretending to be a dog for hours is more challenging. Fetch, tickling, and tummy rubs only last so long. Pink Dog, like a real dog, didn't talk. Olya only barked answers to anything I asked or said. When I asked what she wanted for lunch, I only got, "Woof, woof." I worked out a one-bark-for-yes and two-barks-for-no system and asked very strategic questions. Ham? Nutella? Cheese?

By the time Ron came home, Olya had worn out the knees of her jeans. I told Ron about my day with Pink Dog and told him, "I know Pink Dog is going to come to you, and when she does, you have to touch her." Ron, discouraged from so many prior attempts, said, "No, she'll just call me 'Malo.'"

As I predicted, Pink Dog came into the room on her hands and knees, jumped onto the sofa, and crawled onto Ron's lap. Ron sat with his arms stretched out wide on the back of the sofa. From prior rebuffs, he knew even an accidental touch would get a "malo" from her, so he wasn't chancing it. The only touching she tolerated from him was when she initiated tickle time. She was a worthy and fierce opponent in the giggly game. Or when he carried her into the house after she had fallen "asleep" in the back of the car. No matter how short the trip, she would be asleep when we got home.

From the sofa across from them, I pantomimed and mouthed, "Pet her!" He mouthed back, "Nooooo," too discouraged to take the risk. After more encouragement from me, he mustered the courage and stroked Pink Dog's head. She responded by pressing against him like a cat does. Ron melted. Within a week, our family was back to just one dog, and he was brown. Olya didn't need Pink Dog anymore.

Smudge was a great friend to Olya. He really helped her adjust.

27. Too Many Questions

(Pippa's story)

Michael won the award for the most questions. We were both on the board of the local advertising club and, for several years, had run into each other at meetings and events. I really liked him and his wife, Lauren. They were the kind of people that, when you were around them, you just smiled.

Everyone was curious and asked lots of questions about our experience adopting Olya. I didn't mind answering the same questions over and over because I was so excited to have found her and be her mother. Michael's questions, though, went beyond passing curiosity. I had an inkling he and Lauren might be considering adoption.

Long before we ever left for Ukraine, I had mentioned to Ron that we should invite Lauren and Michael to dinner, but we never got around to it. Since we didn't know them that well, it was a little awkward to ask. Now we had a good excuse. "Would you and Lauren like to come to dinner, meet Olya, and look at our pictures from the trip?" "We would love to!"

Olya charmed Lauren and Michael. We had told her they might be interested in adopting a little girl from Ukraine, so when we showed the pictures on the big screen TV, she pointed at things she thought important for them to see. The next day, Lauren called and asked if I would go to lunch with her. While we were eating, she said, "I'm sure you've already guessed, but Michael and I want to adopt. We are in love with Olya and want to go to Ukraine and do everything just the way you and Ron did." I knew it!

Within the year, they were back with their two kids, Nastia and Sashi. We invited them to dinner again. Soon after, Nastia wrote this essay about her best friend.

Best Friend

I have lots of friends but my best friend is Olya because she was nice to me and she played with me and she is from Ukraine like me. She was nice to me when I first came here to America. We played games on the TV in her house. I knew how she felt when she didn't have a mommy and daddy in Ukraine. She is special to me because she likes to have fun with me, and she knows how I felt when I was in Ukraine.

Privyt Olya! (Hi Olya).

Lauren and Michael Gold visiting with their newly adopted children, Nastia and Sasha.

28. Do You Have a Son Who Has a Sister Named Olya?

(Pippa's story)

We knew Olya had two brothers because her orphanage had told us, but we didn't know if she knew she had two brothers. At dinner one night, we asked her if she had brothers and were excited when she said, "Yes, two." Wanting to know more about what she remembered, we asked her their names. She said, "Erik and Tony." Those were the names of two of Ron's grown sons, not her biological brothers. She had given us the answer she thought we wanted to hear.

A few days later, we were more specific and asked if she had two brothers named Andrewska and Dima. Olya answered, "Yes!" When we asked her if she would like to talk to them, she lit up with excitement. Now we had to figure out how to find them!

We knew the town in Spain where Dima lived with his adoptive family, and we knew their last name. We asked one of our Spanish students, Pedro, to call the Spanish operator to see if he could find their number.

After hearing about Pedro's special mission, the operator stayed on the line and, instead of giving Pedro the standard two phone numbers, gave him the numbers of everyone in Zaragosa with that last name. Then, on a whim, the operator gave Pedro one more phone number for a family with an odd spelling of the same name.

We prepared a list of six questions for Pedro to ask whoever answered the phone. He called eight numbers, but no one answered "yes" to the first question, "Do you have a son who has a sister named Olya?" There was only one more number on the list, the number for the oddly spelled name. It wasn't the last name the orphanage had given us. Pedro called, talked for a few seconds, and then started shaking. We knew the person on the other end of the line had said "yes" to the first question. We had found Olya's brother!

Pedro asked the rest of the questions, and Dima's father answered "yes" to everything but the last. He didn't think Dima was ready to visit with Olya in the summer but did agree to let the kids write, share pictures, talk on the phone and meet someday. Ron and I were so excited to be able to give Olya back such an important part of what she had lost.

We learned from Dima's parents, Jaime and Cristina, that, through the Chernobyl Children's Program, Olya had spent two Christmas holidays and two summers in Spain with another host family in Zaragoza, Spain. The two families were acquainted, and the children had played together on weekends. There was the answer to why our Ukrainian daughter spoke Spanish and who the Spanish Mama had been.

Dima's parents brought him to see Olya in 2002, the first summer she had been our daughter. We all went to Disney World.

The kids saw each other in Spain and the U.S. many more times. This is the Whytes second visit to the States. Pictured: Pippa, Moose, Ron, Smudge, Jaime, Cristina, Olya and Dima in 2004.

29. Forever

(Pippa's story)

Time to eat. Hot, don't touch. Are you cold? Let's go. The first conversations we had were functional. I had heard from another mother who had adopted a seven-year-old Ukrainian child that it took about six months before a child learned English well enough to discuss feelings and abstract concepts.

Of course, Ron and I knew that Olya would be our daughter forever, but we didn't know if she knew it. "Forever" wasn't a concept I could explain to her in English, and even if I had been able to explain forever in Ukrainian, Olya probably wouldn't have understood. She hadn't ever experienced forever. The only consistency in her life had been inconsistency. She had already lived in the village with her biological family, in an orphanage with both brothers, in Spain with neither brother, in a different orphanage with one brother, and now in the US with us. She had learned that relationships and situations are temporary.

Olya and I were in her room playing when I thought about the three of us being a family forever and the feeling of security that could bring her if she understood. I knew she wouldn't relate to the concept of having us as a family forever, so I tried to think of a more tangible way to explain it. I told her, "You know Smudge will always be your dog. Your room and bike (purple with streamers on the handles) are yours forever, and Dad and I will always be your parents." She clapped her hands together and squealed, "Yay!"

A month later, her little classmate, Maria, was over for a play date. Kim, one of my favorite students, was watching the girls when she overheard Maria say to Olya, "I wish I lived in your room." Olya explained, "My parents looked all over Ukraine for me. Maybe someday somebody find you." Olya had repeated to Maria the story we had told her of her adoption to make her feel special. She was using her story to encourage Maria, but Maria already had two terrific parents (her mother was the beloved cleaning lady at our school), a sister, and a brother. The only thing Maria didn't have was a floor full of toys and a bedspread with matching curtains.

Smudge, Olya, Ron and me at our turn-of-the-century farm in the north Georgia mountains in 2003.

30. Why you pick her?

(Pippa's story)

After cleaning out their garage, my parents came for a visit. Even though I told them I didn't want the trophies I had won as a teenager, they just couldn't throw them away without double-checking with me one more time. As my mom and I carried the big box of trophies out to the dumpster behind our condo, she explained to Olya, "Your mommy won these when she was a girl." Even though they weren't as shiny as they had once been, Olya was very impressed with my trophies and asked my mom, "This why you pick her?" Olya thought every child was "picked out" by parents. My mom didn't know what to say. "No" wasn't the right answer, but "Yes" wasn't either.

Olya went on to win plenty of her own trophies. She became one of the top high school softball players in South Florida.

74

Growing up, Olya was great at all sports, including gymnastics. She could do the rolla-bolla, a board you stand on while balanced on a cylender, but here she is lifted above another gymnast's head who is on a rolla-bolla. She had to keep her body perfectly stiff in order to not throw off his balance.

Olya (middle) and her friends in a gymnastics show. I created the sets and painted them with the help of the other mothers. Ron, Olya, and I had seen Lion King, which inspired the giraffes.

31. Again Can Almost Take Forever

(Andry's story)

When I was twelve, I was really into technology and cell phones, and I kept talking about a certain phone that I wanted. One day, Emilio said, "Tomorrow, we will go to the train station to get the phone." I remember thinking how random it was to go to the train station for a phone. I rode my bike everywhere and had seen the phone at stores that were much closer to the apartment, but I had never been to the station on my bike. I thought the deals might be better there. Emilio knew better than me.

At the train station, I walked through the hall and talked with Emilio. I was excited. He said the phone store was only a few doors ahead. That's when I saw a kid walking toward us that reminded me of Dima. I never spoke much about Dima, but I told Emilio, "That kid looks like my brother." Just as the boy passed, Emilio said, "Andry, he IS your brother." It was a surprise they had planned for me. His father had brought him to Cordoba to visit overnight. Dima had changed since the last time I saw him in Ukraine at the orphanage, and it was so unexpected to see him in Spain.

I kind of froze at first. I felt weird when I saw him three years ago in Ukraine because he had things. He had parents. Back then, I was just in the orphanage, obeying the rules but having nothing. In Spain, we were kind of equal. I had Emilio and Milagros, and I had a brother and sister, a house, clothes, and the things a normal kid would have. But I was kinda a dick. Dima and I spoke for a few minutes, and then I asked Emilio, "Are we still getting the cell phone?" He said, "Another time."

We went back to the house and met up with Milagros, Jesi, and Jony. Dima and I played PlayStation. Then someone gave me a video camera, and I decided to do something silly. I wrapped myself up in a blanket and pretended to be a gypsy street vendor, and Dima was the customer. There were lots of shoes in the room, so we lined them up, and he would ask how much the shoes cost. I would answer, speaking Spanish with a gypsy accent.

At dinner, I remember not wanting Dima to leave. I told him, "It's still winter break. Why can't you stay, or why can't I go with you?" I started crying at the table. Something had gotten in my head about him leaving and never seeing him again.

Emilio called me to the kitchen to see why I was upset. Then Dima and his father, Jaime, joined us. I explained I was upset because I didn't want Dima to leave. Jaime reassured, "We will see you again." "When is again?" I asked. "Again can almost take forever." Jaime said, "Next summer." He couldn't lie about something like that. That would really be playing with my emotions. I believed his promise and felt better. Hellos and goodbyes are always hard for me.

Dima and me at the train station, seeing each other for the first time in four years.
I was 12 and Dima was 10.

My brother and me playing with a remote-controlled car at a park in Cordoba, Spain.

32. The Question

(Pippa's story)

We had been together in Fuengirola, Spain, for three days, and the families were on a happy high from reuniting the kids. We had been at the zoo and were walking back to the hotel. Ron, Olya, and I walked behind Cristina, Dima's mother, and Milagros, Andry's Spanish host mother, who were speaking in Spanish to each other.

I remember Andry was in front of them walking his tough, little walk. He turned and started walking backward so he could face them. I could tell he had asked Milagros a question, and she had carefully explained something to him. Then he asked Cristina, who smiled and nervously laughed a little as she responded. I could tell both women had said "no" to whatever he had asked, so Andry turned and hurried to catch up with Dima, Jaime, and Emilio.

Since I don't speak Spanish, I asked the mothers what Andry had asked them because I thought it had to do with the next activity. I am more adventurous than they are, so if he wanted to play basketball or putt-putt, I would be happy to take the kids. Dima's mother speaks enough English for us to limp through a conversation. She told me that Andry had asked each of them if they could adopt him.

He was twelve, about 5'3" and 70 pounds, and he wanted a different future.

33. His Future – Her Past

(Pippa's story)

Our little family was happy: vacations in the mountains, art and gymnastics classes, softball games, play dates, and dinner together every night. On Sundays, we had Mermaid Morning. Olya and I would go to the beach and play Bucking Seahorse. While Olya held on piggyback style, I would bounce and dive in the waves until she lost her grip and tumbled off. She'd beg to ride again and again until I was exhausted. Then we would head to the beach and dig a hole, bury her up to her neck, and I would build sandcastles around her head as the passing tourists giggled and took pictures. Tuesday and Thursday evenings were her special time with Ron. He taught her to play softball. Quite the athlete, she learned to catch anything and outthrow all but one of the boys her age. When she drew pictures of the family, our clothing was always decorated with hearts, and sometimes, she drew our hair in rainbow colors. Our house in her pictures had heart-shaped windows and door, a rainbow over it, and a big yellow sun smiling in the sky.

I didn't think much about the psychology behind Olya's drawings until I was at the house of her little friend, Melissa, whose parents were going through a divorce. Melissa's drawings were such a stark contrast to Olya's colorful creations. Melissa's drawings of herself, done in pencil, depicted her as quite small next to a giant house that didn't have any doors or windows. Her mother said the psychologist they were taking Melissa to had explained that Melissa's drawing showed she was feeling overwhelmed and depressed.

I was pretty sure I knew what the psychologist would say about Olya's drawings.

Why should we risk our wonderful family dynamic by adding an almost-grown stranger to the family? Andry was bound to have bad ways. Knowing something about his childhood, it was to be expected. He might be aggressive, steal, do drugs, or worse. But what if he just needs a chance? I thought about the feral kitten our yellow lab had found on my birthday in the alley behind our building. In the beginning, Birthday Cat, as Olya named him, misunderstood feeding time and would attack our hands when we filled his food bowl. No one had ever given him food. Until we took him in, he had to fend for himself, competing with the other strays for dumpster scraps. With time, consistency, and patience, Birthday Cat developed into a pretty cool cat whose unique personality kept us laughing.

If we didn't adopt Andry, we knew his future was probably bleak. He wouldn't have many career options. According to statistics, most boys from orphanages joined the military or turned to a life of crime. Not able to bear the thought of Andry in Ukraine leading a hopeless life that we could have prevented, we knew we had to adopt him.

In giving Andry his future, it occurred to us we would also give Olya her past. She remembered almost nothing about her life before we adopted her. She was a mystery to herself.

Because of Ron, she had become the most photographed child on earth. She only had one early photograph of herself at an orphanage dance performance - a frilly dress with a big white bow stuck on top of her head. Olya still had her name but had lost her heritage, language, memories, and childhood with her brother. Here was our chance to give her back one of the many things she had lost, Andry. He could give her the rest. He knew what the village was like where they spent their first years together. He would remember what caused the terrible burn on her bottom and down the back of her leg and explain her memory of swimming in potatoes.

This drawing is of the family under a rainbow: Olya, Pippa, Ron and Pippa's parents (Olya's grandparents), Cara and Jim. Olya drew this when she was six and had only been in the U.S. for a week. In the beginning, she always drew herself next to "Mama".

Olya drew this a year later. She explained the family is at the farm. I am wearing overalls with lots of pockets and high heels. Dad is wearing his zebra suit. (note: Ron does not own a zebra suit.) Olya often drew hearts on our clothes and had started drawing herself between Ron and me. We hoped this meant she felt loved and safe.

Olya at 20 standing next to her childhood artwork. She was in 5th grade when we bought a new refrigerator. When it arrived, the white front door panels I had selected were missing. Clever Ron saw the opportunity. He had me collage the front of the frig in Olya's art. Then he made clear plexiglass, door panels that protected her drawings. I bet the appliance company could have sold a lot of these to parents with young children.

34. Easter In The Village

(Andry's Story)

Every year, for Easter break week, Maria would pick me up from the orphanage. Then, we would stop by to see Hallah, Hannah's sister, in Kiev. The next day, we would figure out how to get to the village. If she had been able to save money for the trip, we would take a train, to a bus, to a *marshutka*, a kind of small bus, and then, if we were lucky, someone would give us a ride, most of the way to the village. If she didn't have money, it meant a lot of begging and a lot of walking. At the marshutka stop, she would talk to the driver and explain that she didn't have enough money and that it was just her and the boy. Most of the time, they let us on, but I would have to sit on her lap, or we would have to stand since we didn't pay as much as the other passengers.

Easter is a big holiday in Ukraine. People spend days or even weeks getting ready. They make Pysanky, which literally means "little writings". Villagers, using wax, draw different symbols or designs on eggs that have had the yolk blown out of them, and then they dip the eggs in different colors of dye.

Designs are based on the wishes they have for their neighbors, friends, and family. Pysanky with leaf, fruit, or rake patterns symbolize a good harvest and might be given to a neighbor. After all, everyone in the village had a small garden where they grew their own food. Other designs include a spiral pattern, which symbolizes longevity. A flower - a beautiful life, a sunflower - fertility, and a geometric star pattern is for protection. The tradition dates back to pagan times and is probably where Easter eggs originated. I don't remember Maria decorating eggs. I believe Hannah did it because she was home alone. I would only have a week for that holiday so all the preparations were made before I got there.

The Sunday after Easter, *Hrobki*, everyone walked to the cemetery carrying a bag in each hand filled with food for lunch along with candy and Pysanky to give as gifts. To get to the cemetery we had to walk through the field behind our house where we grew vegetables, but in May, it was too cold for anything but potatoes to be planted because they could handle a freeze. Then we walked along the narrow trail that was the property line with the neighbor's garden, uphill across two other people's property to the road. We lived close to the cemetery. The walk took less than 10 minutes.

When we got to the cemetery there would be people who didn't live in the village. Since the collapse of the USSR, when collective farming ended, there weren't any jobs in the village. After graduating from high school, young people left for nearby towns looking for employment. At Easter, they would come back to visit and bring their children to see their grandmothers. They would park their cars on the grass around the entrance to the cemetery. Most people in the village still drove a horse and wagon. The few villagers with a car had a Loda, a Russian car nicknamed *kopiyka*, a penny. The cars parked at the cemetery were much nicer, so I knew these people were not from the village.

When we got there, Hannah would sit on the bench that every family plot had for this occasion while Maria removed the leaves and weeds from our family's graves. The family name was Buzenok, which means elderberry. There were three graves: Hannah's mother's, father's, and her son's. He had frozen to death as a toddler, before Maria was born, and was buried between his grandparents', my great grandparents' graves.

At the time, I didn't know the custom of Hrobka dates back to the middle ages. Ancient people would visit the graves of their deceased relatives and feast together with them. They believed the dead loved hearing warm memories about themselves.

I also didn't know that fifty feet from the family plot was the village's mass grave, where several of Hannah's siblings were buried when they were children. They had died of starvation, along with 30% of the villagers in Telizhyntsi, because of a famine created by Stalin. It was so bad that inside the post office, there was a sign that said, "Don't eat your children." People walking down the street fell over dead from starvation. Since there weren't enough healthy people to dig graves for all of the dead, the mass grave was dug with a tractor.

Stalin purposely caused the *Holomodor*, which means death by starvation, to force collectivization. Most Ukrainian citizens were self-sufficient. They lived on land that they owned and farmed and didn't want to turn their land, homes, animals and farm equipment over to the government. To break them, Stalin ordered that all the grain be taken from individual farmers and sent to Russia. If a farmer held back grain to plant the next year as punishment, he was sent to Siberia.

Hannah, who was born just after the Holomodor, was given the name of one of her older sisters who had starved. She told me that when she was little, the family survived on turtle soup, tree bark, and edible grasses. Anything that would take the hunger away.

After our three family graves were cleaned, Maria would lay a blanket on the grave closest to the walkway and fill it with as much candy as she had been able to afford. Other families would be sitting on the benches by their graves. Parents would give their children bags and tell them to walk to the different family plots. When a child approached a grave, they would say Hrestok Voskres three times, Christ has risen. Christ has risen. Christ has risen. Then, the child would open their bag, and a family member at that grave would put candy in the kid's bag. The child would then move to the next grave.

It is best to walk around to the graves with a friend because then you aren't as shy, but I had to do it alone because I didn't have Olya, Dima, or my friends from my orphanage, and I wasn't close anymore, to the friends I had had in the village. Based on the style of the grave, I knew where I would get better candy. If the grave had a fancy cross or gravestone with a picture or statue, the family would have enough money for a fancier candy. My favorite was a white chocolate ball covered in coconut that they didn't sell in the village. It had to be bought in another city instead of the little market in the village that only sold the cheap, little candies that we, along with the other villagers, bought.

After the children walked around all the graves collecting candy, they went back to their own family's plot. Then, each of the families and the families around them would gather at a nearby picnic table. There were many tables scattered throughout the cemetery. Each family would put out the food they brought: deviled eggs, sausages, cheeses, sliced cucumbers, bread, salo and always vodka. The adults would talk and toast for a couple of hours and catch up with each other. I was a kid and couldn't care less. It was boring. Then, most people would pack up their graves, but some people would leave candy or a shot of vodka for the dead. For me, that's when the fun began.

Maria, Hannah, and I would go back to the house and look through my candy. At dusk, when I thought everyone would be gone, I would get my bag and go back to the cemetery to collect the candy people had left. Sometimes, a few families would still be packing up, so I would hide behind a grave or bush until I saw them leave. Then, I would get just as much candy as I had collected while walking around the graves during the day when it had been appropriate. I was curious about the shots of vodka, so I took a sip of one. It burned my mouth, and I regretted trying it. I don't remember ever seeing another kid in the cemetery at night, but I was the poorest and most unsupervised in the village. When it got dark, I would get some kind of uncomfortable feeling, like someone was watching me. Maybe because I knew I was doing something wrong. The feeling would disappear as soon as I walked through the cemetery gates and headed home. I didn't feel like I was doing anything that wrong. If I hadn't gotten the candy, the ants would have eaten it, or it would have been ruined by the rain.

I'm showing where my great grandparents are buried and where the family celebrated Hrobki, when the children go to gravesites in the village cemetery to receive candy. In this photo, I am
13 and about to be adopted.

35. I Have No Future in the Village

(Andry's story)

When I got back to the orphanage after spending the summer in Spain, I told Dennis, Maxim, and Vasiliy that my sister's family had come from the U.S. and offered to adopt me. I could go live with my sister in Miami. The guys were excited for me. Soon, the rest of my class and teacher knew, and then the grade above and the grade below me.

The Americans had said they would come in a few months, but they didn't. My classmates believed me, but the rest of the school thought I had made up the story. Most of the kids that got adopted went to live in Italy and Spain. No one had been adopted and gone to the U.S., so my story sounded fake. I knew the Americans were coming, but I didn't know why it was taking so long. Spring came and passed, and still nothing.

I always spent the Paskva holiday back in the village. For some reason, Maria and Nikolai didn't have the right to come pick me up at the orphanage, and they knew it. Maria usually came with a fake uncle or godfather, so the orphanage would let me leave with her. That time, it was just Maria. We took a bus to Tetiev and then another bus to a village a little past ours because there wasn't a bus that stopped in Telizhetsi. Our village was too small.

I needed to tell Maria about the Americans, but Maria and I are both private. People would overhear us talking if I told her about them on the bus. The two-hour walk to the village would be a good time to tell her about the Americans' adoption offer. I knew she wouldn't be mad because life would be better for me if I was adopted. But she wouldn't like me not being around to help her out when she wanted stuff.

While we walked, I explained to Maria that when I was in Spain, Olya and her parents had come to visit me. After the second visit, they asked if I wanted to be adopted and be with Olya. Maria wanted to know what I had told them. I told her I had said yes. Life would be much better for me with the Americans. If I stayed in Ukraine, I wouldn't have anything. After graduating from the orphanage, I would just go back to the village and do labor for the rest of my life unless I found a taste for alcohol. Then, I would turn out that way.

I was her only child left in Ukraine. Now that I was leaving, too, she didn't have anyone to rely on. She couldn't rely on Nikolai. She couldn't rely on Hannah. There wasn't anything Maria could say, so she stayed silent. She only asked, "When is this happening?" I told her I didn't know, but maybe summertime.

I knew the Americans would bring Olya when they came for me. It had been six years since Maria and Nikolai had seen her. They would want to see her again, but I didn't really want Maria and Nikolai there because something weird might happen. Maria might get emotional, which might make me change my mind. I told her, "If you come to see Olya, you can't say 'hi' or anything." Maria answered, "Of course not. We don't speak the same language. It's not like I'm going to talk to the Americans and convince Olya to stay with me. I want to see her from a distance. She probably won't even recognize me." I agreed to let Maria and Nikolai know when the Americans were coming.

At the beginning of June, I had to make a choice. Should I go to Spain or stay at the orphanage and wait for the Americans? My friends were all leaving for Spain and Italy. My teacher told me a couple of times I should go to Spain and give up on the Americans because a lot of kids think they will get adopted, and they don't. She had never met the Americans. I knew if I went to Spain, I would miss them if they came, so I stayed and hung out with the kids I wasn't good friends with. We went fishing and jumped off the river bank into the water and stole raspberries, cherries, and apples from people's yards. Time went by quickly. Soon, I received a call from the U.S., and the translator, who spoke to me in Spanish, told me the Americans were coming in two weeks and gave me a date, June 27th.

Maria and Nikolai came early in the morning the day the Americans were to arrive. They hadn't come to see me leave. They came in hopes of seeing Olya. The three of us went for a walk around the town. They bought me ice cream. We waited on the Americans for a couple of hours. They waited on the bench on the sidewalk in the front while I went with my friends. We climbed on the roof of one of the buildings at the orphanage because it was easier to reach the mulberry branches. Plus we liked climbing things. Even if we could have reached the berries from the ground, we still would have climbed because the berries were thicker and richer at the top, where no one had yet picked.

Some kid came to get me from the office. Each of us at the orphanage had a job. Some helped in the kitchen, setting up tables and setting them with silverware and drinks. Other kids supervised the goats. Others acted like a receptionist, taking different shifts in the day. My friend was covering the office. I told him, "Get me if the Americans come." Then, I kept checking in with him whenever I changed locations. Since I had told him where I would be, he found me quickly. As I ran to the office, I told Maria and Nikolai that the Americans were there. I had planned to walk by them with Olya so they could see her, but it didn't happen that way.

Maria, Nikolai, and me in the village the year before I was adopted. The photo was taken with the camera Pippa and Ron gave me so I could document my life in Ukraine. I would have pictures to remember my family and friends by, when I moved to the U.S.

36. The Meeting

(Pippa's story)

When I first saw my future son, he had berry juice all over his face, and his fingers were dyed red. Excited to finally see each other, we hugged, but it was awkward. As that long-awaited moment ended, I looked around the large, dimly lit orphanage lobby with its seen-better-days furniture and large Soviet-style murals. Through the window, I saw two people in the distance sitting still and emotionless on a bench next to the sidewalk. Even though I had never seen a picture of them, I recognized the couple. The man had Andry's dark hair, and the woman had his long face and lanky build. I told Ron, "They're here." We had known there was a chance that Andry's biological parents would show up, but we had no idea how they would react to us.

Nikolai, the father, had a history of violent behavior. Before she even learned English, Olya, whom we had adopted five years earlier, had pantomimed for me a memory of seeing Nikolai punch Maria in the face. When I asked Olya, "What did you do?" she put her fingertips under her eyes and slowly ran them down her face. She had cried.

We were concerned for our safety and considered hiring a bodyguard for our visit. Instead, we decided kindness might be the best strategy and, if worse came to worse, there is strength in numbers. Between Ron and me, the driver, the translator, and my parents, surely Nikolai wouldn't try anything.

As Ron and I walked outside to greet them, we didn't know what to expect. Feeling anxious, I thought, "Nikolai isn't any taller than I am.

If I have to, I can take him." When we got close, we smiled, stuck out our hands, and, with a positive tone in our voices, said things like, "It's really nice to meet you. Olya and Andry are great kids..." We knew they wouldn't understand our words, but they would understand our smiles and friendly body language. Both Maria and Nikolai looked meek and fearful. They showed no ill will toward us. They just stood and stared, studying us, not knowing what to do.

From behind me, Olya watched them. I could see Maria's desire to touch her daughter, who now considered her a stranger. Olya had only been three when she was removed from her biological family and put in an orphanage. She didn't recognize Nikolai or Maria and barely remembered Andry and the village where they were born.

To help ease the tension, I told Olya to show them how good she was at cartwheels. Her gymnastics coach back in Miami Beach called her his little Russian because she had such a graceful, athletic build. Showing off for them would allow her to interact without being close enough for them to touch her, which would have made her uncomfortable. They acted impressed, and as Olya performed, we had the translator tell them details about her life with us. Six years had passed since they had seen her. She had changed so much since they last visited her in the orphanage when Nikolai threatened to kill her and anyone who adopted her.

We didn't know exactly why the Ukrainian government had terminated Maria and Nikolai's parental rights. The records simply said they were not good parents. Even though the two didn't deserve Olya, they had still lost their daughter, and we felt for them. Every delicious moment we shared with Olya meant they had missed that time with her. Over the years, as I tied pink bows on Olya's ponytails, tucked her in at night, or taught her how to catch fireflies or squirmy tadpoles, I had thought of Maria. Did she even know what she was missing? Would these moments have been as precious to her as they were to me? Having anticipated the possibility of meeting Olya's biological parents while we were in Ukraine, Ron had prepared a photo book of her years with us, but he hadn't brought it with him to the orphanage.

Maria and Nikolai knew we had come back to Ukraine to adopt Andry. Andry was the one who had told them we would be at his orphanage that day. While Maria and Nikolai waited for us to arrive, Andry climbed on the roof of the orphanage so he could pick the berries on the top branches of the tree that the younger kids hadn't been able to reach. Seeing their daughter again and meeting us, her new parents, and their son's future parents had been important to them. They had ridden a bus for two hours in order to meet us that day.

When Olya's gymnastics performance ended, Nikolai started talking. His voice was low, tentative, and monotone. Our translator explained that he wanted us to promise to keep Andry in school and to bring him back each year to Ukraine to visit. Maria didn't speak or smile. At first, I thought she was shy, but then I realized she was trying to keep her mouth closed so we couldn't see that she didn't have teeth. She was probably ten years younger than me, way too young to be missing all her teeth.

The first meeting had lasted long enough. The pauses, where we smiled and silently looked around, were getting longer and more frequent. There was nothing else to be said. We took a group picture. Then, just before Maria and Nikolai headed to the bus station to catch a ride back to their village, Nikolai asked another question. Would we come to visit them in the village, Tilejezy, and have lunch?

Ron and I agreed to go but questioned if we really should. We had been cautioned about getting too close to the biological family. We had a good feeling, though, because everything had gone well in our first meeting. This was an unexpected chance for Olya to see the village where her life had started, and sharing this experience with Andry would be a great bonding opportunity for all of us. Ron and I were curious about what seeing the village would tell us about our children. When we visited, we could give the biological parents the photo book Ron had made for them of Olya's last five years with us.

As the pair disappeared down the long, tree-lined sidewalk, Ron and I discussed how empty they seemed, but maybe that's how they always were.

Olya, my mom, Kristina the translator, my dad, amd me in the orphanage lobby waiting for Andry. Ron was taking the photo.

Outside the orphanage a few minutes after meeting the children's biological parents. Andry is taking a photo of Olya with Maria's phone.

Andry, Maria, Olya, Nikolai on the bench outside the orphanage, 2006.

Maria and Nikolai leaving the orphanage to catch the last bus.

37. I Am an Orphan

(Andry's story)

When I came back from being in Spain for the summer, I expected to go back to my old orphanage. Instead, I was taken to a new orphanage. The one I had been in only went up to kindergarten, so I started first grade at Pereyaslav Hmelnitsk.

One building had three stories and was for schooling. They had nice books. Education-wise, it was great. The second building was the dormitory and cafeteria. The building looked like what you see in movies showing USSR prison cafeteria scenes. Life there felt like it was in black and white.

On weekends in the summertime, two classmates, who were both named Roma and I, would go to the bazaar that was next to the orphanage. The bazaar sold everything from goats to Playstations, but we were most interested in stealing bb guns. I didn't like stealing, so I would distract the vendor, who was usually a grandmother-type person, by asking questions, and Roma would steal the gun. A lot of strategy went into it. Stealing three guns at the same time would be too noticeable, so we only stole one gun per Saturday and rarely from the same vendor. We wanted the guns so we could play a Fortnight-style game against a group of boys in the grade above us.

Roma was great at drawing. When we were on our break from class, he showed me a map he had drawn of the whole orphanage, including the basketball court, soccer field, orchard, outhouses, river, trees, bushes, and school buildings. I was fascinated at how detailed he had drawn everything.

You could actually tell trees and bushes apart because they looked exactly like the real ones. The map was our advantage in beating the other team because we could mark out our positions and make a plan.

School ended at 3:00, and dinner wasn't until 6:00. Between that time, we weren't supervised. We could roam the property and do whatever we wanted, play basketball and soccer, go eat apples in the orchard, but that's not what my friends and I did. We were a bunch of seven and eight-year-olds shooting at each other with bb guns. When we played, there was no way to cheat because when you got shot, it hurt. I don't remember anyone crying, but when you got hit, you didn't want to play anymore.

During the Christmas season, there is a tradition called Kolyadki. It is similar to Paskva, where you walk around to graves, recite a saying, and receive candy, except for Kolyadki, you walk to peoples' apartments or houses. When I lived in the village and did this, I mostly received candy. The people in Pereyaslav, since it was an actual city, were wealthier, and most of them gave money.

Kids had to learn a long saying to recite. It went like this:

A good evening onto you, lord, your lordship!
Now rejoice! Oh, rejoice you earth,
The Son of God is now born!
Do lay out the tables
With your finest linens
Now rejoice! Oh, rejoice you earth,
The Son of God is now born!
Do set out the kalachi,
Baked from the spring wheat,
Now rejoice! Oh, rejoice you earth,
The Son of God is now born!

After going door to door all morning and reciting that, I went back to the orphanage and spread out all the candy and money on my bed and counted the money. There were a lot of coins and a few bills. With that money, I was able to buy food because the orphanage didn't give out extra portions, and what they gave us was never enough. I would buy Mivina (the same thing as Ramen noodles), swipe a pan from the kitchen, build a little fire outside, and make an after-school snack. I wouldn't have turned out to be a good person if I had stayed in that school. There weren't enough rules. I needed more structure and supervision.

Sometimes, Maria and Nikolai picked me up from the orphanage to spend long weekends with them in the village. They were taking me back one afternoon and decided to first stop by the supermarket across from the school. Inside the store, one of them told me to take some things and hide them in my puffy coat. I wasn't doing it for me; I was doing it for them so they would have something to eat on their trip home. By car, the trip only took two hours, but they didn't have a car, so it was quite an ordeal to get home. They had to take a combination of an *elektrichka,* a small train, bus, or *marshutka*, a small bus/van, and hitch-hike the last portion of the trip. The trip would take five hours if they were lucky.

One of them signaled me to head to the exit of the store. As I got to the door, a security guard in a black leather jacket asked me to show him what was inside my coat. I was going to make a dash for it, but I knew he would catch me. I started pleading with him, saying the food was for my grandmother, who couldn't walk, and that I was just helping her. He grabbed me by the arm and took me to the office where the security cameras were. I had never seen cameras in a store before. In the little village store, there was just a babushka staring at you as you walked around.

The guard showed me the footage of me taking food, looking around, and then putting it in my coat. The guard wanted me to tell him where my parents were so he could contact them. I told him I was an orphan and lived across the street in the orphanage. He called the orphanage, and my teacher walked over to pick me up. I thought I was going to be in a lot of trouble, but actually, she was just very quiet for the 10-minute walk to the orphanage. I asked if I was in trouble. She said no, she was disappointed in me. That she knew that I knew better. Her being disappointed made me feel worse than being yelled at or spanked.

As we walked back to the orphanage, I saw Maria and Nikolai standing in the distance, next to an apartment building, and watching me. I obviously didn't tell the teacher about Maria and Nikolai and that they had asked me to take the food for them. Now, thinking about it, I was probably meant to be a distraction for them because they were also taking things. That's why they had me walk out first. If the guard was busy with me, they could easily take things and walk out of the store without being caught.

At the end of the next year, the school had some problems, I assume they were financial, and my grade and everyone in the class below me were transferred to other orphanages that had space. The grade above me made fun of us, saying they were grown up, but we were little kids, and we had to go. I'm glad I didn't stay in that orphanage. The chance of doing well or even okay, having grown up in that orphanage, wasn't very high. The next orphanage I went to in Bucha was like heaven compared to my second orphanage.

*This is my second grade class photo. Our wonderful teacher is on the back row.
I'm on the front row with my knee up.*

38. Teeth

(Pippa's Story)

We were over the middle of the Atlantic Ocean, eating airplane food, when my tooth broke. Olya, Ron, my parents, and I were only a few hours away from seeing Andry. We had told him it would take us about six months to come and adopt him, but it had taken a year longer. Some of the kids in the orphanage had even started teasing him, saying we weren't coming. We had desperately been trying to get to Ukraine, but in 2004, the country experienced presidential electoral fraud, which resulted in the Orange Revolution, where over a million people protested in Kiev's Independence Square. The government shut down, and all adoptions, even simple ones like ours, where a sibling was being adopted, were put on hold. After surviving multiple assassination attempts, which just increased his popularity, the pro-democratic Victor Yushchenko won the re-vote for president. Soon after, we received permission from the Ukrainian government to come adopt Andry.

When we flew into Ukrainian airspace, our excitement grew. We were so close. We were about to see Andry! It had been a year since Olya, Ron, and I had visited him in Spain, where he spent summers with his host family. My parents had never met their future grandson and asked us lots of questions about him. Talking made my tooth pain worse, but talking with everyone about our plans was all I wanted to do.

We decided as soon as we landed, we would immediately dump our luggage at our apartment and go see Andry. I hoped, right after that, we could find a dentist. I had broken a molar once before, but it wasn't painful. This time, the broken tooth felt like a shard of glass. My tongue was actually bloody from rubbing against it. I had found some chewing gum in my purse and wrapped it over the sharp part of my tooth. It was challenging to keep the gum in place, but at least I had some relief.

When we got to the orphanage, we were surprised the director said we could take Andry with us. When we adopted Olya, we were only allowed to see her for two hours a day until she was legally our daughter. By contrast, Andry was permitted to stay with us while the adoption got finalized, which, we had been told, would take about two weeks. Little did we know the process would take seven long weeks and be filled with laughter, amazing bonding opportunities, scary experiences, and heartbreaking stories.

We had met the kids' biological parents when we were at the orphanage, and they invited us to their house in the village, for lunch the next day. This was an amazing opportunity to see the village and house where Olya and Andry had lived before the orphanages. Finding a dentist would have to wait!

The next day, we set out for the village, which is about an hour and a half south of Kiev. The Volkswagen van was pretty crowded: the driver and translator in front, Olya, Andry, and Ron in the second seat, and my parents and me in the third seat. An hour or so out of Kiev, we left the "interstate" and started driving on smaller roads. Olya and Andry sat with computers on their laps playing Simms 2.

The Ukrainian countryside is idyllic, with row after row of tall, thin poplar trees forming windbreaks in the gentle, sloping, sometimes flat, very fertile fields of wheat. Once in a while, a cow or two. Now and then, a horse-drawn wagon loaded with beets or potatoes. The sky was sunny with wind-blown clouds and a morning temperature in the seventies. A perfectly beautiful day. From out of the van window, as we were speeding along the narrow roads, Ron took photos. The blue sky, over the large fields of yellow wheat, was an exact replica of the Ukrainian flag: a large panel of blue over an equally wide panel of yellow.

We stopped in one of the mid-sized towns to buy presents for the Burlaka family. Our translator told me Burlaka, Nikolai's last name, which became *the children's last name, means 'to carry a heavy burden.' We found a very small version of a Walmart, perhaps more like a flea market of shops side by side with everything under one roof. We decided to buy two cell phones for Maria and Nikolai so they could communicate with Andry after he came home with us to Miami. Andry picked out the two phones with cameras, and we bought a big package of minutes for the phones. We went across the street to another shop that sold meats and bakery goods and bought chocolates for the kids' maternal grandmother and paternal grandfather, who we knew would be there to meet us.*

After another half hour of driving, the road was very small and Andry was directing the driver where to go. He began to point out the places near the family house – where he fished, where Maria worked for ten minutes in the morning and evening feeding someone's pigs. Soon, we would be at the house.

When we stopped and got out of the van, within a minute, we were surrounded by a dozen sturdy babushkas. Obviously, Maria had told her neighbors the Americans were coming. They were all excited to see Olya and had been watching for us out of their windows. These old ladies, in their flowered kerchiefs and equally flowered dresses, called, "Olya, Olylinka, Ollichka", all nicknames for Olga, and passed her between them. Olya was very patient and let them all hug her, rub her face, and stroke her hair. Several of the babushkas said something to me in Ukrainian while touching a hand to the inside crook of their opposite arm. Our translator told me they were saying, "I remember when Olya was this big." This was the first time in seven years they had seen Olya. One babushka turned out to be Olya's biological grandmother, Hannah, who talked in a steady stream to anyone who would listen. Maria had rushed from the house and joined the crowd, staying to one side and beaming at Olya and all the attention she was getting. Nikolai also joined the group.

Maria was always smiling but never opened her mouth. Our translator suggested her teeth may have been knocked out, something they frequently see if there is an alcoholic husband. I remembered the story Olya had pantomimed for me before she spoke English, of Nikolai punching Maria.

Once Olya spoke English, she no longer remembered the story, so I never knew exactly what had happened.

Ron brought out the Iphoto book of photos he had made of Olya and another book of Olya, Andry, and Dima when we were together in Spain the summer before and gave them to Maria. She held on to the book of all three children, but the larger book of Olya was quickly snatched up by the babushkas. My parents turned the pages for them, narrating, in English of course, which was Greek to the group, but no one seemed to mind as they pointed and sighed and squealed in a steady stream of Ukrainian, each person talking rapid-fire at the same time.

It's impossible to describe the emotional impact. This was the first time the villagers had seen Olya since she was taken from the village when she was only three, but it was obvious that her return enraptured these old women.

Maria requested that we go up to the house, because the grandfather, Nikolai's father, was there in a wheelchair, unable to come down to the reunion. We pulled Olya out of the babushkas' clutches and followed Maria to the house, where she shyly invited us inside. The interior was extraordinary; every inch of wall space was covered with religious icons, old framed B&W photos of family members in traditional Ukrainian clothing, calendars with brightly colored pictures, lots of faces of women from magazine pages, embroidery, and large intensely patterned carpets. The effect of all this imagery was garish but beautiful as well; this house was a piece of art, "outsider art," but art for sure.

Olya had been curious about her past. While in Miami, she had asked me if "the people" in Ukraine would have baby photos of her. Through the translator, I asked Maria if she had any. She pointed to a stack of four small photo books on a table. She stood by as I went through the photos with Olya. They were mostly photos of Andry when he had gone to Spain with the Chernobyl Children program, undoubtedly brought over the years to Maria by Andry. There were also a few photos of Olya, probably taken by her Spanish host family and given to Maria by Olya's orphanage.

Ron and I call Olya "the most photographed child in the world."
We always have a camera pointed at her, documenting every smile,
accomplishment, and special moment that we can. (Soon, Andry will also
experience this.) It's hard to believe the visual record of these children didn't
begin until they went to Spain when they were four and seven. There are no
photos of the times when the children were living in the Ukrainian house.
They have no baby pictures of themselves. Of course, Maria and Nikolai
would not have had a camera nor the means to make prints; this is now a
very poor place.

Also sitting on the table were large framed photos of the children, which
we recognized as the ones we had sent Andry while he had been waiting
for us to come to adopt him. We realized he had been bringing the photos
to Maria and Nikolai. Andry told us many times that he wanted to be
adopted by Ron and me and live with his sister in Miami, but at the
same time, we could see the strong bond he had with his biological parents,
or at least Maria. It was obvious how important it was to him to have his
biological parents meet his new parents. He was the one who "orchestrated"
the meeting at his school the day before, even though the plan had been for
them to see her from a distance.

As far as we could tell, the house only had three small rooms and a
cubbyhole-like space where food was cooked on a gas burner. I couldn't get
into that space; it was filled with two women bent over preparing food. The
room with the table of pictures had two twin beds, with colorful spreads
pushed against the walls, a red cabinet, and a chair. A few potted plants
were on the window sills, and a dozen jars of fruits and jam were stored
against a wall.

Maria and Nikolai wanted us to see everything and seemed pleased
that we took so many photos. There was no embarrassment; Maria especially
seemed proud of her home. It was very neat and orderly, even if the floor
was seriously sagging, and a large tree limb helped support the ceiling.
She pointed out the place where Olya and Andry had slept. We had seen
this unique type of heated bed in the houses at the historic village we had
visited, when we had come to adopt Olya. An interior wall of the house had

a woodburning stove built on one side and a clay, shelf-like structure the size of a twin bed built on the other side of the wall. Under both the stove and the bed, there was a space where you could place wood to cook or warm the "bed" that had blankets spread on it to make it soft. We also heard how Hannah had once rushed the children outside when the bed started smoking.

Being in the village was like walking back in time. Maria was born in the house, and Hannah before her. The house had been built by the children's great-grandparents. Olya and Andry's great, great grandparents had also owned the property, but lived in an older house that was torn down to build the current house. Five generations, maybe more, had lived and farmed this acre of land. To this day, the house does not have running water. Water for cooking, washing, and bathing is brought from a well in the front yard that is shared by several neighbors.

My father pointed out a dilapidated outhouse about 15 feet from the back of the house. Andry told us they couldn't use it anymore and pointed to a small stand of trees they used instead. I wondered how that worked when there was three feet of snow on the ground and no privacy because the trees had all lost their leaves.

While we were having a tour, a neighbor friend of Maria's and an aunt of Nikolai's had been continuously taking food outside to a table under a pear tree, where silently, Nikolai Senior, the grandfather, sat in his wheelchair. Old Nikolai, to us, looked younger, than younger Nikolai. The old man was in a suit coat and collared shirt. His face didn't have the ravaged look of his son, as if he had spent his life indoors while his son toiled outside in the weather. We were told Nikolai senior had killed his wife, and that is why Nikolai, the kids' father, had been sent to an orphanage. Maybe Nikolai Sr. had spent a good part of his life indoors because he was in prison for murder. The women pulled some rickety-wobbly benches around the table and motioned for all of us to sit. Our translator, Yelena, said they hoped we would join them as their guests for a little meal they had prepared for us, but the meal was no little thing. On top of a flowered pattern vinyl tablecloth, there were two large bowls of mashed potatoes with fried onions on the top;

several dishes of cucumbers and tomatoes; a large bundle of bananas; slices of orange; a bottle of wine, another of vodka, another large bottle of beer, a plastic carton of lemonade; slices of bread; and a plate of cured meats and cheese, a bowl of wrapped chocolates and a dozen flies on top of each dish.

The interesting thing is that no one was given a plate or napkin. Instead each person was given a large spoon, the idea being for everyone to reach across the table and scoop out and eat what they wanted from the different serving bowls. Think of it as double-dipping on steroids.

Getting everyone to the table had been chaotic, but it finally happened. In addition to our driver, translator, my parents, Ron, and me, there was Hannah, Nikolai's father, Maria's friend, Nikolai's sister, her husband, and occasionally Maria when she wasn't jumping up to get something. However, Olya and Andry spent most of the time in the house. Andry was putting together the pair of cell phones we had brought to Maria and Nikolai, so Andry could keep in touch with them from the USA. Olya was looking at photos of herself when she was younger and in Spain on the Children of Chernobyl program. Now and then, she would rush out to the table to show Ron or me a picture because it had sparked a memory, then run back into the house. On one trip out to us, Olya whispered in my ear and asked if Maria and Nikolai ate the chickens that she had seen in the pen in the front yard. I told her that they did. I explained that they had to grow most of their own food. She looked worried and asked me if they also ate the puppies and kittens that she had been playing with.

The women all urged us to eat more and more, but we noticed that Maria hadn't eaten at all. When we asked why, the women said that Maria never ate; she just worked. None of us could drink enough vodka to satisfy them, either. Ukrainians do a toast that consists of three consecutive shots. I spent an hour nursing one shot and managed to toss another over my shoulder when no one was looking.

The conversation at the table was a steady stream of everyone talking at once. Yelana could not keep up with the translation. Slowly, the conversation turned to Olya. The aunt, Nikolai's sister, was a little aggressive, something we had not seen from anyone else. Apparently, she was saying that she didn't know what was wrong. The children had plenty to eat and many people around to take care of them. She went on to say that when Maria signed a paper terminating her parental rights, she had believed it was only for three months. I'm not certain the aunt, who lived in a different town, had been told the whole story. Neither Ron nor I responded except to say we know how heartbroken they must have been, but I'm not sure our response got translated. The dialogue got lost after that.

We asked Maria to tell us some stories about the children when they were little, but she didn't seem to want to or just wasn't able to do that. It sounds like things got rude, but they didn't. It was a sad atmosphere more than angry. I didn't get the impression that they blamed us. After all, they had gone to a lot of trouble to receive us. They spent money that they couldn't afford to spend. Yelana helped us out, telling everyone that we had to get back to Kiev by 6:00. The aunt asked if we could give her a ride to the next town. We did one more round of photos of all of us. Ron said that now we were one family; they were part of ours, and we were part of their family. That seemed to please them. We quietly gave Yelana money to give Maria to cover the cost of the feast.

We tried to collect Andry and Olya. Olya was sitting on the stoop with one last old babushka, complete with a walking stick that doubled as a fire poker, who had finally made her way to the celebration. The woman mistakingly held the wrong end of her stick, and Olya's face was covered in soot where the old woman had caressed Olya. I wiped her face, and my mom sat down next to Olya and the sooty-handed babushka. Maria rushed back with a cloth for my mom to sit on so she wouldn't get her pants dirty on the less-than-pristine bench. As poor as this household was, we had the impression that Maria was fastidiously neat, a characteristic we see in Olya.

Everyone hugged goodbye. Before we left, Maria gave me a gallon jar of cherries and another of jam that she had put up from the fruit that grew around the house, and she was saving for the winter when they didn't have fresh fruit and vegetables. We piled into the Volkswagen van, waved to the crowd in the street, and drove away from where our daughter and, hopefully, our new son, Andry, had lived. It was as if we were driving out of the pages of a history book in the section on "Peasants of Rural Ukraine."

That night, when Ron and I were alone, we reflected on the day. Undoubtedly, the children were better off in an orphanage than they were being raised in the home of their biological parents. However, it happened, and we may never know the exact details. It was for the best that Nikolai and Maria had their parental rights terminated, but we still felt for Maria. We could see that she really loved and wanted the children. She just couldn't provide a healthy and safe environment for them.

Losing your children has to be the worst thing a mother can experience. I wondered, what if I had been born to a single mother in a poor rural village, had limited education, no resources or opportunity, married at 18, had my first child at 19, and the man I married turned out to be the kind that was violent to me when he drank. Would I have had the where-with-all to change my situation? It was easier for me to think "yes" before I met Maria and saw her life first hand.

Ron and I wondered what we could do to make Maria's life better in a long-lasting way. I don't know who came up with the idea, probably Ron. He always had good ideas, but we both agreed. We would offer to get Maria new teeth. She was only 32 and was missing all of her front teeth. She didn't really smile, talk, or eat with others. You could see how self-conscious she was. Having teeth would make her feel better about herself. Nikolai had missing teeth, too. If we didn't get him teeth, would he be jealous of hers and be more likely to hit her in the mouth? The next day, we had Yelana call Maria to see if she would let us take her to the dentist to see about getting her teeth. We extended the offer to Nikolai too. They accepted. I thought maybe I could get my tooth fixed, too.

The next day, our driver and translator picked us all up in his unairconditioned VW bus and drove to the village where Maria and Nikolai squeezed in, too. Years later, when Andry spoke English well, he told me what Maria and Nikolai were saying to each other on the drive from the village to the dentist's office. Maria was very nervous about going, and Nikolai was telling her, "Don't be scared. This is a good thing. This *isn't something you could have done on your own. Don't look nervous and mess this up."*

Andry, freaked out by the process that was about to take place, chose to wait in the van with the driver while the rest of us went inside. The dentist's office, like most of the buildings outside of Kiev, did not have much grass or landscaping beyond trees that had been planted decades before. Tamed weeds grew on each side of the sidewalk. The double doors of the dentist's office stood open, and a cat walked in ahead of us. The lobby felt cheerful with floor tile the color of Dijon mustard. While Yelana, along with Maria and Nikolai, spoke to the receptionist, the rest of us took seats in straight-back chairs that neatly lined the wall. Two dentists in white lab coats walked by us on their way to their examining rooms. Instead of shirts under their coats, you only saw chest hair. Was this because the summer day was one of the hottest on record? The hats they wore were like the white, paper ones worn by butchers I had seen in U.S. grocery stores.

Maria and Nikolai each had their consultations with the dentists, and appointments were made for their upcoming procedures. After seeing the large metal syringes in an examining room and the 1950s-era dental instruments, I decided against an appointment for myself. That night, when we got back to our apartment, I found my nail file and took care of my jagged tooth myself.

The next week, we took Maria and Nikolai back to the dentist for their follow-up appointments. He was only missing a few teeth, but she was missing almost all of hers. She had to have her few remaining teeth pulled in preparation for dental implants, where prosthetic teeth attached to screwlike posts would be drilled into her jawbone. The process would take several months to complete, so we wouldn't be able to see the finished result before we had to fly home. Before we left the dentist's office, we paid the balance of the bill so she could complete the process and made her promise to send us a picture of her smiling.

When we got back to Miami and settled in, I encouraged Andry to stay in touch with Maria. Once a month, I had him call her. While she was always excited to hear from him, he had to carry the conversation because she never asked him questions about his life, and to his questions, she never gave more than one-word answers like "fine," "okay," or "not bad." There would be long periods of silence when he couldn't think of anything else to say.

During the calls, he would have a death grip on my wrist to make sure I stayed next to him. He would mouth to me, "What do I say next?" I would write notes to him on Post-Its like, "You can tell her about your wrestling match and your science fair project on feral cats." I would also write questions for him to ask her, "What did Hannah do today? What are you growing in the garden?" Questions that might start a longer conversation. Several months later, she came through when she sent Andry a selfie over WhatsApp. In the photo, she had a big smile, and we could see her new teeth.

The neighbors came out to see Olya and the "Americans" (Pippa, Ron, along with Cara and Jim, Pippa's parents) when we visited the village in 2007, when we were in Ukraine to adopt Andry.

Olya and Andry sitting on the bed where they slept as children. Traditional Ukrainian beds share a wall with the kitchen's wood-burning stove, which keeps the bed toasty.

Maria put a lot of effort to prepare a feast to celebrate our visit to the village.

Olya, with a lap full of puppies, sitting next to an old woman from the village.

The children's grandfather, Nikolai's father, who murdered his wife, is on the far right in a wheelchair beneath the tree. From left to right: Cara, Nikolai, Andry, Ron, Maria, Olya, Jim, Pippa and Hannah. Notice Maria's arms around the kids. The photo gave her a chance to pull them close to her. It had been five years since she had seen Olya.

39. Oktober Hospital – No Celebration

(Pippa's story)

The adoption was final! Andry, Olya, Ron, Kristina, our translator, Vascilly, our driver, and I were having our celebration dinner at the USSR, the nicest restaurant in Kiev that we knew of. The place was decorated to look like a traditional village house with a thatched roof, thick stucco walls, and paintings of flowers on the walls. The waitresses wore traditional red patterned skirts, white poofy shirts, and garlands of flowers and ribbons on their heads. We were happy, eating great food and making toasts, saying "Smudgenoho," which means cheers in Ukrainian. We teased that we couldn't say that back home because our chocolate lab, Smudge, would get upset at being told "no" so much.

We were enjoying all sorts of delicious dishes like cherry verineky and salat vinaigrette (beet salad) when Ron got up and went to the restroom, or so I thought. After what was too long, I asked Andry to go check on him in the men's room. When Andry didn't find Ron there, he asked one of the waiters if he had seen him. Ron had gone outside.

Andry rushed to get me, and with Kristina translating, he told me that Ron was lying in the parking lot, and two strangers were with him. They had called an ambulance. Zoom, we made it outside just as the ambulance pulled up. Ron was on the ground, curled up in excruciating pain. I knew from experience that Ron was having a gallbladder attack. To make the situation even scarier, he also had a bad heart. The year before, when Ron had a gallbladder attack, his doctors had been worried that the pain would trigger a heart attack, which was even more serious.

The medical team quickly got Ron into the ambulance, and Kristina and I climbed in after them. Or at least I tried to get into the ambulance. They blocked me and said, "no". I told them, "I'm his wife"! The attendant responded, "No wife," and closed the door in my face. I clung to the outside of the ambulance, trying to see through the little window in the door, and begged Kristina to get them to let me in.

Ron was not in a condition to be able to answer a lot of questions. I knew what was wrong! I knew his medical history and that he was allergic to codeine. It would be a disaster if they gave him codeine to try to help his pain. After a lot of pounding on the door, it opened, and the same man who had pushed me out of the ambulance called to me, "Wife." I was in!

Ron was on the gurney with the two medical technicians doing stuff all around him. I quickly told Kristina what was wrong and that Ron needed morphine quickly. Each side of the ambulance was lined with shelves, totally empty shelves. I remember thinking our bathroom was better equipped with medical supplies than the ambulance was. Fortunately, the ambulance had one thing our bathroom didn't have: a small glass vile of morphine. The medical technician broke the vile in half and drew the morphine up into the syringe. Within moments, Ron had stopped screaming from pain, and we were headed to Oktober Hospital, a very large facility on a hill. Vascilly and our TWO children followed the ambulance in his old school, green VW bus.

Who knew you had to bring your own sheets when you went to the hospital! Oktober Hospital had other surprises, too. The ER doctor spoke English, was very Westernized, and had a great bedside manner. He had on jeans and a white lab coat and looked very much like Ron's son, my stepson, Tony, which put us at ease. Tony's doppelganger doctor sent us upstairs with a nurse for an x-ray. The elevator was actually a small room with a table, chair, and telephone. We wondered, with such a quick ride up or down, who had time to sit and relax for a phone call.

As the nurse wheeled Ron down the hall, he flipped a light on and then off for each segment of the trip; otherwise, the floor was in total darkness. The style of the furniture was from the 1950s, and the x-ray machine, the size of a double bed, was from the same era. During our three-hour stay, Ron was the only patient we saw in the entire hospital. The place was surreal and reminded Ron and me of the movie The Shining, but instead of the isolated Overlook Hotel in Colorado, it was the isolated Oktober Hospital in Kiev.

After viewing the x-ray and doing a physical exam, the doctor confirmed that Ron's gallbladder was the issue. The doctor offered that they could either operate the next day or give Ron morphine (in those odd little glass bottles) and syringes to take with him in case he had another attack before we could get home. Ron opted for morphine and surgery back home.

At the celebration dinner, Andry, Olya, and I waited for Ron to return from the men's room, but he didn't.

The hospital elevator had a table, chair, and 50s-era phone. The hospital was huge, but Ron was the only patient we saw. The halls and rooms were empty.

40. Going Home

(Pippa's story)

Good news. Olya was back with Andry, just like things should be. Now we just had to get him home. Bad news. There wasn't an available seat in the coach until Wednesday, three long days away. We had been in Ukraine for seven weeks and couldn't stand the thought of being there one more second than was absolutely necessary. We bought a last-minute, $2,000 first-class ticket back to the States.

In order for us to adopt Andry, Ron had been required to come to Ukraine, but it had been a big health risk because he suffers from deep vein thrombosis. (Though I am sure he would have come anyway, not wanting to miss the experience or risk something happening to Olya or me.) Olya and I flew coach, but Ron had flown first class so he could move around easily, elevate his legs, and help his circulation. Both kids had flown back and forth to Spain without a parent next to them, but that was then. Ron and I decided to each ride with a kid instead of the two of us being in first class with the kids together in coach. Since Andry had bonded most with me, we thought he would be most comfortable sitting with me. Olya was excited to sit in the "fancy section," as she called first class.

I put my seatbelt on. We were finally safe and on our way back to normality. I felt this immense sense of relief pass over my body. Exhaustion and sleep overwhelmed me. As I breathed heavily and closed my eyes, Andry said, "You sleep?!" After a short pause, I opened my eyes and said, "Of course not!" While I was spent, he was understandably excited and energized to begin his new life.

"Want to see where your room is?" I drew floor plans to explain the layout of all the rooms in the house. Then I drew a map of our town showing everything important: our house, where he would go to school, the beach, park, pool, where Ron and I work, and Olya's school. I described the extended family with words and cartoons and drew his new, complicated family tree, complete with the spelling of everyone's names. We spent almost the entire eight-hour flight talking. He was learning English so fast.

This 13-year-old boy, whom I knew so little about, was now our son. During our time with him in Ukraine, his fluctuating moods had the rest of us on an emotional roller coaster. Why did his moods change every five minutes from hateful to helpful, interested, playful, and jealous? He had survived so much and been shaped and molded by so many factors I knew nothing about. What was he thinking? Would he ever see us as parents, or were we just a ticket to a better life? As we talked, he tried to tell me about his life in the village, the orphanage, and in Spain, but because of his limited vocabulary, it was difficult for him to express himself. After hours of conversation, he said, "I not know you love me until you cry." I was shocked he had put that feeling into words and shared it with me. He had just given me a tiny piece of who he was.

The day before we left, I was taking out the trash and asked him to help me. He immediately snarled, "Why me?" I was hurt by his tone and reaction. We had come all the way across the ocean, spent thousands and thousands of dollars, endured a health crisis, and taken seven weeks off of work all for him, and he couldn't help me take out the trash! Unlike the other times he had made me cry, this time, I did not hide it from him. I stood there in the middle of the kitchen with tears streaming down my face.

Ron explained to Andry that he needed to hug me. Andry walked over and stood one inch from my face. I buried my face in his shoulder, took his arms, one at a time, and wrapped them around me. He was stiff, but it was definitely a hug, and he was doing it willingly. It was what I had needed and probably what he needed, too. After holding me for a few seconds, he stated, "I finished." "I'm not," I replied and held him for a couple of more seconds before letting him go. We both smiled in relief at our joke. Then we took out the trash.

The movie had not been working, but toward the end of the flight, Blades of Glory started showing, and we laughed together at the silliness. You didn't need to understand the dialog to understand the movie. After a while, Andry put his pillow against my shoulder and fell asleep.

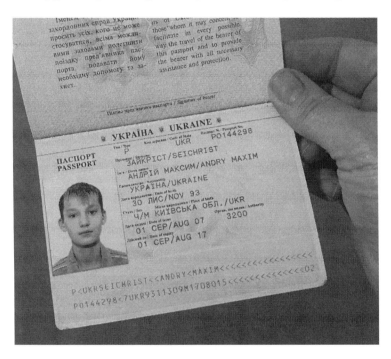

It had seemed like forever, but Andry was finally our son and had our last name to prove it.

41. Just Try Your Best

(Pippa's story)

Before we brought Andry home, he was worried about two things. Making new friends and getting good grades. Through our interpreter, I asked Andry, "Do you have friends here?" He said he did. So I explained, "You're a good guy. You will have friends in Miami, too." About your grades, Dad and I don't care if you have Ds and Fs. As long as you do your best, we will be proud of you."

Back in the States, we enrolled Andry in school so he would repeat 7th grade. He just knew a tiny bit of English. We thought learning brand new material and English at the same time would be overwhelming. On his first report card, Andry had As, Bs, and a C in math. I told him, "What is this, C?!" Surprised at my reaction, Andry said, "You said it would be ok if I had Ds and Fs." I hugged him and said, "That was before I knew how smart you are!"

On his next progress report, Andry's B in science had gone down to a D. Ron and I grounded him. Andry couldn't watch TV or play video games unless it was with the family. He had to read a page from his science book every night and then tell me what he had read. As Andry heard he was grounded and we explained what being grounded meant, a huge smile slowly covered his face. All he said was, "Okay." Ron and I were surprised. That wasn't the reaction we expected from him. We had expected him to refuse, to huff off and slam a door. Then we realized what he heard us say was, "We care about you." He had heard exactly what we were saying.

After that, Andry brought home 14 straight As on every assignment and test. He told me, "You're the only person who ever helped me with homework." We realized how important it was to him to have us believe in him. We needed to set the bar high for Andry because he had the ability to get there. He just didn't know it.

Andry started school in the U.S. as a 7th grader. His science project on iguanas made it to the country fair.

42. I Have Everything I Want

(Pippa's story)

Lixa cried every single day of 2nd grade. The tears started as soon as her older brother, Carlos, left after walking her to class. Their family had just immigrated from Cuba, and Lixa was in Olya's class. The desks were set up in a big U-shape facing the board, with Lixa sitting across from Olya on the opposite side of the room. Each morning, for the first 15 minutes of class, I would help Olya with her schoolwork and make silly faces at Lixa to make her smile.

When the girls were in 5th grade, we found Andry and started the process of adopting him. Lixa's brother, Carlos, still walked her to class each morning. On the way to school one day, Olya asked me, "Do you think Andry will walk me to class?"

Since Olya was already our daughter, adopting Andry should have only taken a few months. The process was much quicker when you adopted a sibling. At least that's what we had been told and what we told Andry. Unfortunately, the Ukrainian government shut down the adoption center in Kiev. Ukraine was in the middle of the Orange Revolution. The people were rioting as the country fought over which president to elect. We heard that if the Russian-backed candidate won, Americans probably wouldn't be allowed to adopt Ukrainian children!

While we waited for the revolution to end, everyone told us not to adopt Andry. Adopting a teenage boy would ruin our family. The bio father had been violent, and the boy might be the same way. After all, he had seen a lot and still had contact with his biological parents. They might have a significant influence on him.

Even though Ron and I were aware of the risk, we knew we had to adopt Andry. We couldn't leave him there with what we knew were limited opportunities for his future. Olya, Ron, and I had started imagining life with Andry. As the months dragged on, my heart ached whenever I looked at Olya sitting in the back seat of the car. Andry was supposed to be sitting there next to her. I could almost see him.

The revolution delayed us for almost a year, but we finally received permission to travel to Ukraine to adopt Andry. As soon as we landed, we drove straight to the orphanage to see him. With Olya, we had only been allowed to visit her two hours a day until her adoption was final. To our surprise, the orphanage director gave us permission to take Andry with us to stay in our apartment even though the adoption process hadn't even started.

The apartment we had rented when we adopted Olya was the type of apartment working-class Ukrainians lived in. The building was one of dozens of identical-looking, Soviet-era apartment buildings. We didn't dare venture out without our translator for fear of getting lost. Many days, we had to wait in the apartment without TV, music, internet, or heat, which didn't get turned on until November. We wore our coats while inside as well as outside.

Not wanting to repeat that experience, when we went to Ukraine to adopt Andry, we rented an apartment in an upscale highrise condo in the city center. My parents joined us for the first two weeks, so we got an apartment with two bedrooms, a kitchen, a modern bathroom, and a living room with two big sofas where the kids could sleep. It had internet and a large, flat-screen TV with an English language channel, Hallmark. We could walk to the grocery store, and there was a park in front of the building where we played catch with the kids. When we didn't have to jump through adoption red tape, we went to the movies or the zoo. My dad, the kids, and I would spend hours playing the card game Crazy Eight.

We were excited for Andry to stay with us but were perplexed when he would be having fun and then get mad for no apparent reason. Knowing the violence he had seen, coupled with his frequent, intense mood swings, scared me. Worried about what he might do to us when we slept, I took all the knives from the kitchen drawer and hid them between the mattress and box spring of Ron's and my bed. Instead of sleeping in the living room with Andry, I had Olya sleep on a pallet on the floor next to me, where I knew she would be safe.

Seven weeks later, we were back in the States. He was officially our son, but he was still unexplainably moody. Olya's school started before his, so I dropped her off at school first. That's when she got her wish. Her brother and I would walk her to class. One day, as Andry and I walked back to the car, he stumbled on a small crack in the sidewalk. He paused and said, "Three months ago, if I had tripped like that, I would have been mad all day. Now I have everything I want in life." I knew Andry wasn't referring to physical things like a house or computer. He really meant stability and a sense of hope. "I don't get mad at stuff like that anymore."

Andry and Olya, in front of our house, a few months after he was adopted.

43. Empty on the Inside

(Andry's story)

During the week, Maria worked milking cows on the collective farm. On weekends, she did odd jobs at people's houses. Since she didn't want the three of us walking around the village, she would lock us in the house with Hannah, who was usually drunk.

The house was empty. There was nothing to do. No TV; I didn't even know what a television was. No games. No toys unless I had stolen them. No electricity. At 4:00 in the afternoon, we had to light candles to see around the house.

There wasn't anyone to talk to either. My little brother was different. He was filled with nothingness and fear from the abuse he received from Nikolai. And I can understand. My sister was too young to play with. Everything interesting was outside. Even the toilet, just a hole in the ground with a few boards around it for privacy, was outside.

Once a week, Hannah bought vodka and would hide it in the house. I would find her vodka, re-hide it, and tell her, "I'll give you the vodka if you let me outside." Then I would go all over the village and look at new things. Things I could take. My theory was if someone had two good things, I should have one of those things. The best part was I got to choose which of the two things would be mine.

Nikolai was the popular choice in the village if something went missing. Every few days, someone would show up at the house trying to get back whatever Nikolai had taken: money, wheat, a vase. He took anything that he needed or looked interesting to him. Unlike the other houses in the village, our house didn't have a fence or a gate, but the neighbors would still stand on the street in front of our house, not coming into our yard as if there was a fence keeping them out. If a neighbor, looking for a missing item, saw me outside, they would ask me if Nikolai was home. I would go in the house to "look" for him and tell him which neighbor was outside asking for him. Most of the time, Nikolai would instruct me to tell them that he wasn't home.

Nikolai didn't own anything. The house we lived in belonged to my grandmother. Someday it will belong to me. Hannah willed the house to me instead of Maria so Nikolai wouldn't have any legal claim to it when she died. Hannah despised Nikolai.

Owning something made Nikolai feel proud and allowed him to feel normal for a little while because he had something like other people in our village. Unlike everyone else who worked and saved to own things, Nikolai didn't. Our house was the poorest in the village. When he stole something, the good feeling wouldn't last because he had to hide his new possession. He could only show his prizes off to Maria. She would scold him, but at the same time, she was happy, especially if he had stolen a bag of sugar or wheat that she could use.

Working was what gave Nikolai the opportunity to steal. The USSR had fallen, and the government was dismantling the collective farms which had employed most of the village. The young people moved to Kiev in search of jobs. Most of the remaining villagers were elderly and needed help around their houses and gardens. Whenever Nikolai did odd jobs for them, he had access to their house and property. When they took a nap or weren't watching, he would slip whatever he wanted to take behind a tree or hide it at the edge of their property to be picked up later. Once, I was working with him, and he squirreled away a big bag of beats. He would do his job for people but take something, too.

When I would visit the village on holiday from the orphanage, I would go work with them. I didn't get paid, but the neighbor would usually give me a jar of jelly or something like that and pay Maria and Nikolai. We had to take burlap bags of beats from the underground cellar to be planted later.

He told me to go check on the woman and see where she was, to ask for a glass of water if I saw her. I reported to him that she was inside, so he took two bags of beats and put them on the far side of the field to be picked up when we were done working. We headed home.

What I didn't understand was that he also treated our house like someone else's house. He took the jars of fruit and pickles Maria had preserved and saved them for us to eat in the winter and sold them to get money for vodka.

He was an alcoholic, so he had to drink every day. If he was busy, things were good. He would only drink at night because from morning to evening, he had to work. But when he couldn't find work planting potatoes or chopping wood, the craving took over. He would spend the money he earned and even sell our food and the things in our house to buy vodka.

A couple of times, the neighbors blamed Nikolai for things that I had taken. People didn't even consider that the thief might have been me. I was too young. Nikolai knew if he hadn't taken the item, I had. He got the blame, but he didn't care. He would just tell them, "Go ahead, take it back."

I could see who was doing what. I would climb a cherry tree, pick a safe branch to sit on where there were lots of cherries, and lie back and eat them.

When Hannah didn't give me the keys, I would explore the house. I would climb into the attic and search through clothes even though I wasn't going to wear them because they were too big. When I was hungry, I would try to cook. Once, I was on my tippy toes trying to see what was in the bottles on a high shelf, and an open bottle of pepper sauce fell on my face. It burned like hell. I thought I was going to lose my eyes. But mainly,

I tried to figure out how to get out of the house or waited until Hannah fell asleep so I could take the keys and get out.

I think I was seven in this photograph

44. Red Is For Mean. Blue Is For Nice

(Pippa's story)

Under his breath, so only I could hear, Andry would call me fat, ugly, and bitch. When no one was looking, he would flip me a bird. At first, I tried ignoring him, thinking if he didn't get a reaction from me, he would stop. When that didn't work, I explained to him that it wasn't nice to call me those names; it hurt my feelings. I kept the problem to myself. I worried if Ron knew, he would be angry at Andry for being mean to me. Actually, there was something about the way Andry insulted me that wasn't really mean-spirited. I knew Andry actually liked me. Out of ideas, the next time he shot me a bird, I did it back to him. He laughed, said yeah, and gave me a thumbs up. He was happy. I was bewildered.

About a week later, he asked me, "Are you my friend or my mother?" I silently shouted to myself, "Boy, I just figured you out!" For the last seven years, his family had been the boys he lived with in the orphanage. He didn't know how to relate to a mother. He was trying to relate to me like I was another 14-year-old boy. I told him, "I hope I can be both, but if I have to pick one, I pick Mom. You're going to have lots of friends in your life, but I am going to be your only mother. Maria wasn't capable of being your mother. Your host family in Spain is wonderful, but they didn't adopt you. I will be your mother for the rest of my life."

He didn't stop calling me names, but at least I understood him. His insults were actually affection. I decided to keep a journal. Everything he said to me that was mean, I wrote down in red. Everything nice he said to me, his sister, father, the dog, or a stranger, I wrote in blue. I wrote in the journal every day for two weeks. The pages were red with bits of blue. Back then, he was extremely moody and didn't often say anything nice.

Once the book was pretty full, I started keeping it on the coffee table in the living room. The next time he insulted me, I picked up a red pen and wrote down what he said. He asked, "What are you doing?" "Nothing," I said and casually put the journal back on the table. He could have read what I wrote at any time. A few days later, he said something else mean. I wrote down his insult. This time, Andry picked up the book and carefully flipped through the pages. "When I say something mean, you write it in red, and when I say something nice, you write it in blue. Why do you write this all down?" This was the moment I had been waiting for. I had known he would eventually ask me that question. I explained, "You are so important to me. I want to remember everything about our life together." He never again called me a bad name.

45. Escape Across the River

(Andry's story)

Most of the women in the village were old. When Nikolai stole something from them, they weren't going to confront him. If it was a woman, she would call the cops. He was always on the watch after he stole something. He wouldn't walk on the road where the cops could drive. He would walk the edge of the river. Walking next to the river could get you anywhere you wanted to go.

I would go to the river and get mussels at low tide. I would take them back to the house, light a fire in the winter kitchen, and cook them in a pot. I would wait until the mussels opened, then take them out and eat them. Some mussels were the size of an apple. They were so big I could only carry a few. I wouldn't think ahead to bring a bag with me and had to carry them home in my hands. I wouldn't want to leave the river because there were a lot more mussels to get, and if I left, someone would get the others. I wanted them all to myself.

That day, the water was very low because I was in the middle of the river, and the water was below my waist. Nikolai came up and said, "I'm leaving." The svunir are after me. Svunir means pigs and, just like in English, is slang for police. It wasn't a surprise to me. It was natural for the cops to be after him. I asked, "Well, where are you going?" Across the river was an unfinished house. He pointed that way and said, "I'm going to be staying there. Do you want to go with me?" At first, he held my hand as we were crossing the river, but the water got deeper. I couldn't swim.

I told him, "You have to carry me, or I won't go with you." I hung on his side like a monkey. At one point, he could barely touch the bottom and was mostly swimming. When we got to the other side, our clothes were all wet. We half climbed up the hill, and he built a fire inside the house. We put our clothes next to them so they would dry. He asked me to go back to our house and bring him some salo, cured pork fat, and bread. I remember leaving, walking the long way home along the edge of the river, but not going back. Maria probably told me, "No, he can come get the food himself."

This is the river that Nikolai and i swam across. The elderly woman is collecting reeds to make a broom with.

This is Nikolai and me six years after the "escape" and a few months before I was adopted. My adoptive parents had sent me a camera so I could document my life in Ukraine before I left.

46. The Answer

(Andry's story)

There was a stove in the middle of the outside kitchen, and people were sitting around it. I think it was Maria's birthday. I was sitting on the bench next to Dima, then an aunt, Maria's friend, the woman with the mustache, and a lot of other people. Olya was sitting with us, too. Olya saw a cat and wanted to hold it. She was walking after the cat, tripped and sat on the stove. One of the guys there had a car and drove Olya, Maria, and Nikolai to the hospital. Olya had white stuff like rubber bands on her legs. I didn't see it until the bandages came off. Olya was two.

47. The Secret in the Attic

(Andry's story)

There were two reasons the cops came to the village. Nikolai had stolen something, and someone called the cops on him, or he had assaulted Maria, and I had called the cops. I never saw the police in the village unless it had to do with him. The village was small and didn't have a police station. The police had to come from the nearest town, Tetiev.

The police only caught Nikolai about 50 percent of the time. When they caught him and took him away, it would be almost no time before Nikolai was back at the house. The government works in a funny-bad way. In the U.S., if the cops come and you run away, you are committing another felony. Nikolai ran from the police so many times he should have been sentenced to life in prison. When Nikolai did go to jail, he would only be gone a week, and then he would be back. He always managed to escape from jail.

Ukrainian cop cars are small, all-terrain jeep-like vehicles. They're painted dark green and have white letters on the side doors that say MILITSIYA. When the police came for Nikolai, they would never come full-out because Nikolai would see them and run off and hide in the bushes. In the summer, it's green everywhere, and you can stand behind a bush, and no one would ever see you. He played Hide and Seek with the cops, and he was really good at hiding. When he was a child, the game must have been his favorite.

The police weren't going to run around the village chasing him. When they came to look for Nikolai, they always tried to sneak up on him. He would know they were coming because he knew he had done something wrong.

Sometimes, when Nikolai would do something, and I would question why, he would answer that not everything is fair in the world. "There aren't good guys and bad guys. There are ones that drink and are responsible and ones that drink and can't control it." He said he was one of the ones who would drink and lose control, but he wouldn't try to change. The cops who looked for him were like him. They are assholes too. He always said insulting things about them. Even though they had a job and were responsible, they were still assholes.

For me, what he said made sense because, in Ukraine, most of the people do drink. I would consider them alcoholics. They would go to work and have a normal day, but when they went home, they would start drinking, and some of those who drank would be abusive. Instead of going to sleep, they would get an energy burst. It all depended on how they were raised. When we went back to visit Ukraine, we saw that a lot of my classmates would be fine during the day. At night, though, they would start drinking and start fighting each other. That's how the abuse starts. You can't convince a drunk person that they are wrong.

48. Nikolai Didn't Need Anything Else

(Andry's story)

I was with Nikolai, walking back from someone's house where he had been working. After he had finished, the house owner invited Nikolai to take a few shots, and that led to a few more. Half an hour later, we headed home. It was a mile back home, and Nikolai walked like there was ice on the road, like he was ice skating for the first time. I've never seen someone that drunk. "Look at you! This is embarrassing. Let me help you." I tried to put his arm around my neck to help him so he wouldn't fall as much, but he wouldn't let me. Nikolai had an excuse. "The rocks here are too big. I keep falling on them." They were actually just pebbles.

When he was drunk, he would say, "Tomorrow, we should go work at this lady's house. She said she would give us a lot of money." Then, the next morning, he would have a hangover and want a few shots to recuperate from the night before. Those few shots would lead him to the same state he was in the night before. The work wouldn't get done, and we wouldn't have money. Money was important for lights. We always had our lights cut off.

I was surprised. Nikolai knew his faults. But I wasn't surprised that he didn't want to change. He had shelter. (We lived with my grandmother in the house her parents had built.) He had food. He could get drinks. Having anything more was too much responsibility for him. Nikolai did dream big, though. He wanted to have a good family. He would tell me he didn't want to argue. He wanted to be stable, but he didn't realize he had to change to do that.

49. A Couple of Hours Walk

(Andry's story)

The police would drive up and quietly walk into the house to see if Nikolai was there. They wouldn't waste their time if he wasn't. They would leave.

Above the front door was a trap door with a ladder that led to the attic. Nikolai would hide there sometimes and pull the ladder up behind him so they wouldn't think to look up there. The attic was big, the size of the whole house, with two bedrooms and a living room, and it was hot. All the stuff that we didn't use but didn't want to throw away was put up there.

The police would ask Hannah, "Where is he?" She would tell them he was around, hiding somewhere. Since he had gone toward the front door, she would think he had left the house when really he had just climbed up the ladder into the attic. If they had asked me, I wouldn't have told them where he was.

Once, we were going to Nikolai's father's house. I'm not sure how far it was, maybe a couple of hours walk. Once you get out of the village, it's a straight road to the next village. What's interesting about the straight road with fields on each side was a huge square fenced-in area with apple and cherry trees that was about halfway to Nikolai's father's house.

He was my grandfather. I don't remember his name, but I heard he had murdered his wife. That's why Nikolai and his sister were sent to an orphanage. Nikolai kept escaping. He said after you escape three times, they stop looking for you. He used to tell me I should escape. Nikolai's sister stayed in the orphanage and became a hairdresser.

When we walked to Nikolai's father's house, we would stop at the square, sit in the shade of the trees, and get something to eat. Afterward, as we kept going, on the left, there was a strip of trees about a block wide that turned into a forest. It would be an amazing picture from above.

From a distance, we saw a car. At that time, Nikolai was avoiding the cops. From that distance, the car was an ant, so we couldn't see what type of car it was. Just in case, we got on the side of the road and laid down so no one saw us. We did it for every car that went by every 20 or 30 minutes.

Most of the time, we wouldn't get rides and had to walk for two hours, but if Nikolai hadn't done anything wrong, we could put our thumbs up and ask for a ride.

When Maria and Nikolai picked me up from the orphanage for Easter, we could take the bus most of the way home, all the way to Tetiev. From there, we had to walk or look for a ride. While Nikolai and Maria sat at the bus stop, I would stand with my thumb out. Sometimes, if I was playing with a stick or something, Maria took a turn. People were more likely to stop for a child or woman.

I was 16 and had lived in the U.S. for three years. Olya, my mom and I went back to Ukraine to see Maria, Hannah, and the village and orphanages where we had lived. Nikolai, who hadn't been seen in the village for a year, showed up at the house where Maria and Hannah lived, saying he wanted to start a new life. He had a job in another city but needed bus fare to get there. Olya said, "He is just going to drink the money. Don't give it to him." My mom figured if we gave it to him, and he did have a job, he would leave, which would be a win. If he drank the money instead, he would never be able to ask us for money again. We gave him $20.

I told Nikolai to leave the village and get on with his life. The rest of the family had moved on and he needed to also.

The next morning, we saw Nikolai at the village bar, which was just a tent. I confronted him, and, as we knew, the money was gone.

50. Crazy

(Andry's story)

Nikolai liked drinking with a guy who was Hannah's friend's son. He was a big guy with a big stomach. I always stole cigarettes from him. They would be playing cards, and he would put his jacket on the bed. I would go through his pockets and keep the lighter, cigarettes, and coins. I couldn't take the whole pack because he would know, so I just took a few.

He came to the house once when he was drunk, and Nikolai wasn't. He probably wanted Nikolai to go off with him and drink, and Maria probably said no. I do remember the man started being mean to Maria. Nikolai put his arm on him and, in a friendly way, said, "Time to go." The man and Nikolai fought, but the other guy had a knife. They were on the ground, and he was trying to cut Nikolai. It was just me watching the two of them, not knowing what to do. It was so crazy.

51. Pit Bulls

(Pippa's story)

Every morning when I drove Andry to 7th grade, he would ask if he could have a pit bull. I would tell him, "Yes, you can have a dog, but not a Pit Bull." Then, I would carefully explain the two reasons why he couldn't have a pit bull. 1.) We had other dogs and children at the house, and we couldn't have a dog breed in our family that was created to kill. It was too big of a risk. 2.) In Dade County, it's illegal to own a pit bull. Case closed. Pick a different breed.

We are "dog people" and already had two wonderful dogs, a chocolate and a young yellow lab, which we had gotten for his sister a couple of years earlier. Since she had a dog, it was only fair that he should have a dog too. Plus, Andry was having a hard time adjusting to the idea of being part of our family. Maybe if he had to love and teach a puppy how to become part of our family, it might actually help him feel loved and part of our family.

To help him find a different breed of dog, we bought him The Big Book of Dogs, which has large, colorful pictures of all breeds so that he could see what they looked like and read about their characteristics. He still kept insisting on getting a pit bull, saying that he could train it to be nice. That his pit bull wouldn't be aggressive. I would explain that most pit bulls probably aren't mean, but we couldn't take the chance with the lives of his little sister and our other dogs. For generations, pit bulls were bred to fight 'to the death. Even if he trained one carefully, the dog could snap. It wasn't the dog's fault.

After a month of having the same dog debate every morning, I just about had it. I was about to tell him through clenched teeth, "STOP ASKING ABOUT A PIT BULL!" when an idea came to me. Instead of biting his head off, I asked him, "Do you keep asking about a pit bull because Nikolai was mean and aggressive like a pit bull, and you are worried that you will turn out like him? Andry replied, "Yes."

Why hadn't I figured that out sooner? I explained the concept of free will to Andry. "You have the choice to become the kind of person you want to be. A dog doesn't have free will. Nikolai didn't have the opportunities that you have. If you try hard and make good choices, you will be a good person." Andry didn't ask again about a pit bull, and I prayed that nurture, not nature, would be what shaped Andry's life.

Andry did get a dog, a black lab, and a shepherd mix named Chunk. He loved that dog, and the dog loved him.

52. Mom & Dad

(Pippa's story)

We thought that he would start calling us Mom and Dad when a little time had passed, and he felt like the four of us were a family. Six months had passed, and he was still calling us Pippa and Ron. We worried that the first name thing had become a habit for him and he would never get around to calling us the names kids call their parents.

If he couldn't accept us as his parents, he wouldn't develop the feeling of security of having two parents who love and care for your being. We carefully explained that we would like him to call us Mom and Dad. When he scoffed, we insisted on Mom and Dad. He outsmarted us and called us Olya's mom and Olya's dad.

Andry is very smart and asked me a logical question, "How can you be my mom? You just met me." I answered, "Because I decided to be." Before we went to Ukraine to adopt him, we wondered if he would ever think of us as his parents or, since he was coming to the family so late, maybe we would just seem to him like a favorite aunt and uncle. Or maybe he would always feel like he was a guest living with his sister and her parents. Would he turn 30, look back at his life, and feel like he had missed out? Andry needed to decide to be our son.

We understood. Having parents was a new experience for him. Life with his biological parents hadn't worked out. The Spanish foster family he had spent the last six summer and Christmas vacations with had been very good to him, but they hadn't adopted him. Andry had never had a constant person in his life that he could rely on every day, no matter what. He couldn't comprehend that we would always be there for him.

Andry with his second family, the host family in Spain: Emilio, Jonny, Andry, Jessy and Milagros.

Andry with his forever family: Ron, Olya, Andry and Pippa.

53. The One-Armed Man

(Andry's story)

When I was small, before I went to the orphanage, I wanted to work to make my own money. I asked some people, neighbors, what to do. They always said, "Cleaning," and they would pay me with a *hrivna*, which is a buck. I wanted something better. So I went to the man who owned the store. I wanted something to take care of. I wanted to sell ice cream. The storekeeper told me about the one-armed man who worked on his farm. Because the man only had one arm, he needed help. The deal was that I had to stay a year even if I didn't like it, and the one-armed man would feed me and give me a place to sleep. I agreed.

I was supposed to work, but the one-armed man never made me do anything. I would fish, throw rocks at wild hogs with big tusks, and I would lie down in the sun between the rows of tomatoes and eat them.

I helped him sometimes bring the eggs from the place where the chickens had laid them, and I fed the animals. There were many chickens, cows, and pigs. In the barn, I would climb a ladder to where the hay was and sleep there. The hayloft was very cool and as high as the tallest building in the world. When the one-armed man couldn't find me in the morning, he would ask where I had slept. The man said I couldn't take the eggs because he picked them up in the mornings, but I would steal them and cook them over a fire I made with the hay.

For breakfast, he would give me fresh milk and *pampushka*, which is like a crepe. For lunch, traditional Ukrainian borscht. He was nice to me.

Sometimes, he let me shoot his gun. He had a hunting dog. One time, there was a boar, and he shot at it. He had to shoot it five times to kill it. I was next to him. The dog was running next to the boar.

I left after about two months because I got lonely. Maria had visited me several times. The last time I told her to meet me was in the forest close to the house so he wouldn't see her. I wanted to go home, but I didn't know the way. Maria helped me escape.

54. The Black and White Photograph

(Pippa's story)

Hanging in the corner of the main room was a black-and-white picture of a toddler in a coffin. The house belonged to Hannah, Andry's biological grandmother, and had been built by her parents before she was born. Even though Andry had slept in this room until he was seven and had visited several times a year until he was 13 when we adopted him, he didn't know who the child was or really anything about his biological family's history.

Andry was 15; he and I were back in Ukraine to visit his village and his friends in the orphanage. Since he might not be back again for a long time, I suggested he ask Hannah to tell him stories about his childhood and his past. I especially wanted to know the family's medical history. He knew Nikolai, Maria, Hannah, and Hallah, Hannah's younger sister, were in decent health but didn't know about any other relatives. Hannah filled in the blanks.

I expected to hear an all-too-common story of a poor family destroyed by a father's alcoholism and abuse, but Hannah didn't even mention Nikolai. Andry and I could never have imagined the story she would share. She started, "The woman who lives next door killed my mother when she was 78." Hannah's mother had raked a pile of leaves that had fallen from the pear tree on the property line and started to burn them. The neighbor said the fire would kill the tree and told her to stop. The two argued, and the neighbor thrust the handle end of the rake into her mother's stomach. Her mother died two days later.

That morning, I had seen an elderly woman in the yard next door. I asked Andry to ask Hannah if that was the same woman who had killed her mother. It was. Shocked, I asked, with Andry translating, "How can you live next door to her?" Hannah answered, "What choice do I have?"

Maria had been in the other room but heard the story. She came into the room and, in her usual quiet voice, said, "I was glad she died." Shocked again, I asked Andry to ask Maria why she was glad. Maria explained that her grandmother would kick her when she walked by and make her kneel and hold a chair over her head as punishment. Maria had been nine when her grandmother died. Maria was so mild and meek. I wondered how anyone could be so cruel to a child, especially their own granddaughter, and how Hannah could have tolerated her child being treated that way! Then I realized that in this family, horrible things were normal.

Hannah answered Andry's questions and filled him in on the rest of the family. Her father had died at 68 from a heart condition. Hannah had four siblings. Hallah, her younger sister, lived in Kiev in a one-bedroom apartment with her two grown children, their spouses, and two grandchildren. Andry had visited them many times. Her other three siblings had died from starvation when they were children. Hannah was named for her dead older sister. There had once been fields and gardens all over the village, but when she was little, her family had to eat turtles and tree bark to survive.

The day before Hannah told us this story, Andry and I had learned how one-third of the village had been starved in the early 1930s. We had visited his elementary school, where he had gone to first grade, and been invited into a locked room. The walls inside the room were covered with first-hand accounts from villagers detailing how Russian soldiers ordered villagers to turn over their entire harvest, even the seeds they would use to grow next year's crop. If a family refused, the father would be taken away. People walking down the street fell over dead from starvation. Notices hanging in the post office instructed, "Don't Eat Your Children." Russian soldiers even confiscated bread from children's hands and loaves of baking bread from ovens. During the Holomodor, as it's called, Stalin systematically starved eight million Ukrainians because they resisted giving up their land and livestock to the state for collective farming. So many villagers died in Telizhentsi that there weren't enough healthy people to bury them. The bodies were put in a mass grave, now just a depression in the middle of the cemetery, the size of a tennis court.

Andry asked Hannah about the black and white photograph of the child in the coffin hanging in the corner. The child could have been one of her siblings, but the photograph looked more recent. She said she had once been in love. She and the man moved to Kiev and had a son. She wasn't clear, but something happened to the man, so she and the boy moved back to the village to live with her parents. She explained that one day, when it was very cold and the snow was high, a male friend came over, and he and Hannah started drinking. The house got hot, so they opened the doors and windows to cool down. Her son wandered outside. When Hannah and the man realized the boy was missing, they went looking for him. When they found the child, he was blue. He died two days later in the hospital.

Hannah only talked if she was asked a specific question. "Who is my grandfather?" Andry asked. When she was in her thirties, she worked in the office of the collective dairy. A man from a nearby village started finding reasons to come to the office to see her. She liked him, and he said he wanted to marry her, but he didn't. She found out that he was already married and had a family. That man was Maria's father. Hannah said he was still alive, had visited five times since Maria was born, and had even met Andry once. Andry remembered a man he didn't know visiting and giving him a piece of candy.

Hannah had told her story matter-of-factly as if everything that had happened to her had really happened to a stranger. This was the first time I had seen her fairly sober and coherent. Usually, she spent the day sitting on the bench outside the front door, looking out blankly, numb from vodka.

The view across from her bench was of the neighbor's house and tree where her mother had been killed. A few yards to the left was where her son had frozen to death. I wondered if Hannah's countless days on the bench *were spent thinking of those times or if she just watched the ducks pecking at bugs and the sleeping dog that was chained in the side yard.*

The toddler in the photograph was Maria's older brother, who died soon after this photo was taken. His mother Hannah was in the house drinking with a friend when the little boy wandered outside during a snow storm. He wasn't found until it was too late. Hannah's mother is the woman on the left

55. The Nine-Fingered Man

(Pippa's story)

We were in Ukraine because Andry and Olya wanted to go back and see the tiny village where they had lived together when they were little. It had been ten years since the mayor had taken the kids to the orphanage on Andry's 7th birthday. Olya had been almost four and only had a few fragments of memories. She was excited for Andry to tell her stories of their early life and show her all the places they had gone as children.

I think Olya was also curious about Maria, who shared her blonde hair and what she considered fat fingers. Though nothing on Olya was a bit fat. She was so beautiful that the girls on her softball team nicknamed her Barbie, and so elegant that when she walked, it was as if music played.

Life in the children's village hadn't changed since they left or even progressed much since the 1900s. Houses still didn't have indoor plumbing. People got water from a well in the front yard and lugged it back to the house. Horses and wagons, though uncommon, were more common than cars. Our driver's VW bus had broken down so we didn't have a car either. To get around, the kids and I had to rely on our feet.

We walked down the dirt roads and picked berries from the bushes. Women herded ducks using a two-foot twig to prod them along. In the evening, a slow parade of noisy cows, anxious to be milked, plodded by on their way home. Each cow knew which house was hers and would stop at the gate to be let in by her owner. A few wagons filled with milk cans rolled down the street and headed somewhere.

We were busy examining a swarm of red bugs so thick they made the tree they were on look like it was gushing blood when a minuscule, mud-covered, military-style vehicle pulled into the yard of the house next to us. Andry recognized the barrel-chested man who got out and explained to Olya and me that this was the storekeeper who had been nice to him when he was little. The man had let Andry sweep the floor of the store in exchange for ice cream. When Andry had asked for a real job, the storekeeper, who also had a farm, had hired Andry to help the one-armed caretaker do little chores.

Andry called, "Privet," and we walked over to the storekeeper's house. His daughter, who was about 10, ran out of the house and stood leaning against her father, listening to his conversation with Andry. When she realized we were Americans, she looked at Olya and me and said, "Hello, how are you? one, two, three, four, five, six, seven." She was pudgy, with a round, bright face that just glowed happiness. Her father was also gregarious, but there was something dark about him. He was barefooted, and his feet were cracked and filthy. I noticed he was missing a finger.

The nine-fingered man asked Andry if Olya was his little sister. Olya was excited because he was the first person we had met in the village who remembered she had existed. Olya had Andry ask the man what he remembered about her. Andry translated the nine-fingered man's answer, "You looked like a little piece of putty." Next, the man asked if we had ever seen ostriches. He had gotten some ostriches from a neighbor who couldn't afford to feed them anymore and invited us to his farm the next morning to see them. After our busy day of bug watching, seeing ostriches up close sounded like fun.

The next morning, our driver was still stuck in Kiev trying to get his VW bus fixed, so Olya and I walked from Andry's first-grade teacher's house, where we were staying, to the house where Hannah and Maria lived. Andry was staying there along with his friend Ethan. Ethan was a Miami friend who had joined us on the trip.

Olya and I were grateful that the teacher had invited us to stay with her because, although her house didn't have a kitchen sink, it did have the luxury of a bathroom sink and shower. The house also had a toilet, but it hadn't been usable for years. If Olya and I had to go, we had to use the outhouse. The first time we had been to Hannah's house was when we were in Ukraine to adopt Andry. Her outhouse was so dilapidated I thought the breeze generated by the wings of the passing flies would blow it over. Since then, the out-house had been upgraded - replaced by a brick model probably financed by the money we send her for decorated eggs.

When Olya and I got to the house to meet the boys, there were two more kids there: Nastia, the four-year-old girl that Maria frequently babysat, and the girl's short, 13-year-old brother, Denis. Denis had a crush on Olya and watched her constantly through his light blue eyes. Denis and his sister were being raised by their grandmother because his father was in jail for killing his mother. Their grandmother was trying to decide if she should raise them or put them in an orphanage so they might be adopted.

With the addition of Nastia, Denis, and Maria, our group of four turned to seven, and we started on our three-mile walk through the village, over the bridge, and up the hill to see the ostriches. Olya, Andry, Ethan, and I walked and talked. Maria stayed a little way away from us, watching Nastia and shyly smiling at us. Denis followed behind, picking flowers for Olya and occasionally giving one to Maria or me.

At the top of the hill, we saw a large once-paved parking lot of junked cars surrounded by three soviet era warehouses. On one side, between two trees, there was a small table. Two men we hadn't seen before were sitting there with the nine-fingered man. His daughter had been sitting on his lap, but when she saw us, she ran to me and took my hand. The men had been drinking shots of vodka while they waited. It was 10:00 am.

After offering me vodka, the nine-fingered man, through Andry, started asking me lots of questions. He was curious about life in the United States and wanted to know, "Do you have a car? How much does bread cost in America? How many rooms does your house have?" His first questions were easy, but they got harder. "How much money do you make?" I couldn't tell him what my salary actually was because the salary of a fairly successful U.S. business person would have been incomprehensible to him. I told him that many people in the United States make $24,000 a year. I knew that would even seem like a huge amount. Then, before he could ask more questions, I asked him about the ostriches.

The five ostriches were in a room at the end of one of the warehouses. The roof in that section had long ago collapsed and been hauled off, which left the space kind of corral-like. The ostriches stood in thick mud. The only thing edible were the leaves on the other side of the gate beyond their reach.

We probably shouldn't have trusted a man who was already missing a finger when he told us we could feed them; ostrich bites don't hurt. Striking like a cobra, the ostriches reached over the gate and grabbed the leaves along with our hands. Fortunately, the nine-fingered man was right, and none of our fingers got goggled off. The inside of an ostrich's mouth just feels like sandpaper. Feeding the ostriches was fun, but Maria didn't want to try. She usually just observed us from a distance. Nastia was too little to feed them, and Andry was too chicken. He kept jerking his hand back when the ostriches tried to eat the leaves he was holding.

I guess wanting to give us another new experience, the nine-fingered man asked, "Have you ever tasted goat's milk?" "No, I haven't," I replied, and then the nine-fingered man, who was still barefooted, and his daughter ran off to catch a goat. It took both of them to corner the goat, but it was obvious they had done this before. The nine-fingered man pulled the goat's teats until the red plastic cup was filled halfway. At home, I buy the watery, fat-free milk, and the goat's thick, yellowish milk looked disgusting to me. His daughter took the first gulp and then offered me a drink. She looked so cute with her goat's-milk mustache. I took a sip of the warm, yucky milk and politely smiled. Olya, Andry, and Ethan all shook their heads, "No thanks."

Our little group was saying our goodbyes when the nine-fingered man, with Andry translating, asked if we had ever eaten a goat and invited us to a BBQ the next day. Since our driver's car was still broken, we couldn't go visit Olya and Andry's orphanage as we had planned, so we accepted the BBQ invitation. When we asked the nine-fingered man what we could bring, he laughed and said to bring what we wanted to drink. A funny joke since we had rejected his offers of vodka and goat's milk.

Our parade of seven was already down the hill, walking back to the village, when the nine-fingered man called Andry, and he jogged back to the table where the man was sitting with his daughter and two friends. From a distance, I saw Andry lean down, and the man whispered in his ear. Then Andry sprinted to catch up to the rest of us.

When the others were busy watching a cow doing something silly, Andry harshly said to me, so the others couldn't hear, "Why do you always change the plans?!" I had no idea what Andry was talking about. He went on with venom in his voice, "I don't want to go to the BBQ." I was shocked and explained that he had acted like he wanted to go. Since Andry was the only one who understood both Ukrainian and English, he had been in control of the conversation. If he hadn't wanted to go to the BBQ, all he had to do was tell me. Or, since I don't speak Ukrainian and couldn't understand anything the nine-fingered man said, Andry could have just told the man we couldn't go.

Andry was so upset with me. His anger didn't make any sense. This whole trip was for Olya and him. Nothing about the trip was for me. If I had planned a trip for me, we would be someplace that had indoor plumbing, and Ron would be with us. I missed him, but it had been too dangerous for him to come. Since his health was unpredictable, he always needed to be in a country with decent medical care in case of an emergency. I didn't have cell phone service, so I couldn't even call Ron. I was pouting and crying. So the others wouldn't see me, I walked ahead quickly. My head was racing, trying to understand why Andry had so suddenly and irrationally gotten upset. Then it occurred to me. He had changed after the nine-fingered man whispered in his ear. I asked Andry, "Did what that man say,, have anything to do with why you are upset with me?" Andry replied, "Yes." but refused to tell me what the man had said. I knew if I waited, Andry would tell me.

We were halfway back to the village when Denis showed me something in his cupped hand. He had found a baby bird. In the middle of the road was the baby's nest that must have fallen from one of the tall trees that lined the road. Denis put the bird back in his little bed and placed him on the fence post. I had Andry tell Denis that the bird would die if we left him there. We had to take the featherless guy with us. Maria said it was a common bird, nothing special. Probably because Denis saw Olya's interest in the bird, he got him down from the fence. We all looked for worms as we walked back to the village, and I worked on a plan to get Andry to talk.

When we got back to Maria's house, and the others were distracted by the bird, I told Andry I needed to go back to the teacher's house, but I didn't remember the way. Would he go with me? I actually knew the way. I was just trying to get Andry alone. When we were almost to the teacher's house, too far away for him to turn back, I said, "It's not fair for you to be mean to me. I haven't done anything. What did that man say that upset you so much?" Andry stopped walking and looked me square in the face. "The man asked if it would be okay if he had sex with my mother."

Shocked, I laughed and said, "He would have to catch me first, and I am very confident I can outrun him!" I was trying to put Andry at ease by bringing some humor to the situation. He remained serious and said, "You don't understand. If we go to the BBQ tomorrow, he is going to have his two friends there again. Ethan and I can't protect you from THREE men, and Maria isn't going to do anything. She wasn't ever able to help herself. Besides, who would she call? He's the chief of police! Now I understood why Andry was so distraught.

When we reached the teacher's house, we saw our driver's van parked in front of the house. The problem was solved! Tomorrow, we would be able to go on with our original plan to visit the children's orphanage far, far away from the village. Our driver drove us back to the house, and we told the others about the change in plans. I made sure Andry told Maria to call the nine-fingered man and let him know we would not be at the BBQ the next day.

Early the next morning, Maria, the kids, the driver, and I took off on our day-long road trip to visit Bila Tserkva, the orphanage where the children had lived before they were sent to live in three different orphanages. They both remembered how Andry would get permission from his teacher to go to Olya's classroom during playtime. While the other kids went outside, the two would sit on the floor and play with toy cars.

Around noon, Maria received a phone call. After a few seconds of conversation, Andry's eyes blazed red, and he started screaming at her in Ukrainian. The nine-fingered man was on the phone. The goat had been killed and cooked. He wanted to know when we would be there. Maria had never called him to say we weren't coming.

The nine-fingered man with his lovely, vivacious daughter.

An ostrich eating a leaf out of the nine-fingered man's mouth.

Me milking a goat.

The nine-fingered man, his two friends, and the rest of our group.

The group walking back to Maria's house. Andry is angry with me, and I don't understand why. Pictured: Nastia, Maria, Pippa, Dennis, Olya and Andry.

56. Send Eggs!

(Andry's story)

When you look at the village, it's like a reflection of Hannah. They've both been through a lot. Hannah is short, stocky, and everything about her sags; her boobs, eyes, and shoulders. It doesn't matter if it's winter or summer; she always wears the same thing: a long skirt, valenki (winter shoes across between galoshes and Uggs), a coat, and a flowered scarf wrapped around her head and tied under her chin. No one would mistake her for an American. She only has a few teeth. Long hairs grow on her chin. Maria cuts her whiskers when Hannah's sister visits from Kiev or when I used to come from the orphanage on holidays.

Every few weeks, I call Maria and tell Hannah hello if she is nearby. They say I don't call enough, but when we do "talk," they rarely ask me questions or have anything to say. Maria just asks for money.

I get frustrated with her. I tell her, "Remember, if you send Pansanky eggs decorated in the traditional Ukrainian way, you will make more money than you could make doing any other job in the village. The deal she has with my parents is perfect for her. They will buy all the decorated eggs she sends us. Since she has chickens, ducks, and geese at her house, she can easily hollow out the eggs and draw on them. Everybody in Ukraine knows how to draw on eggs because it's a tradition going back hundreds of years. Most of the eggs she sends are really nice. My mom saves her favs and gives the others away to friends and teachers at the school. If Maria sent eggs regularly, I could sell them and send her even more money.

Maria sends eggs every six months but calls me for money every two months. It's hard for me to say no to her, so I try to explain to her the deal she has. If she just decorated one Pysanky egg a day, which would take an hour at the very most, in a month, she could send us 30 eggs and have enough money to live on.

When she does send eggs, I call and give her a code to receive the wire and tell her the amount of money we sent. I encouraged her to send eggs again next month. She agrees. Then, four months will go by, and she calls me and says she needs money. Her excuse for not sending eggs is that she was busy working for other people in the village.

Planting potatoes is one of the few jobs there are in the village. You have to dig all the holes, put in the pieces of potatoes, lug water to put in each hole, and then go back and cover the holes. Then, go on to the next row. At the end of the day, your back really hurts. Maria could make twice as much decorating eggs than she does planting potatoes. Then, she wouldn't have to keep asking me to ask my parents to send her money. No one gets money for free. You have to work for it.

Andry and Olya with Maria, who is showing the Pysanky she made. They are in front of the house that the family has lived in for at least four generations. The photograph was taken in 2006 when we went to Ukraine to adopt Andry.

57. *I Remembered Everything*

(Pippa's Story)

When Olya was a senior in high school, she started asking Ron for the photos and videos he had taken of her over the years. Since I had known him, and before iPhones, he almost always had a camera or video recorder with him. When we adopted Olya, he became even more vigilant about capturing moments.

When she was in elementary school, she also became interested in photography. He gave her one of his cameras, and the two of them would go on photo safaris around the neighborhood. He would photograph her or interesting situations, using a technique called "shooting from the hip" where you don't put the camera to your eye. This way, your subject doesn't know their picture is being taken, allowing the photographer to capture the moment instead of a pose. When Ron was in his 30s, he used this technique to take a series of photographs of people walking in front of a Coca-Cola sign painted on the side of a brick wall. The Virginia Museum bought one for its permanent collection, and another one of the images hangs in our house.

Olya also had her favorite subjects to photograph: car headlights, car back windows filled with collections of objects like stuffed animals or plastic Santeria saints, and dogs being walked by their owners. Her dog photos were my favorite because of her compositions. Her focus was on the dog, so the people would often be partially cropped out of the photo in interesting ways, just like in Ron's photos. I always wondered if she had planned her great compositions or if they were just happenstance. When she and I looked at her photos together, I would ask her, "Which ones are your favorites?" Without knowing the ones I liked best, she picked the same ones.

Ron would have given Olya the videos he had taken of her right away. The problem was he couldn't find them all. He looked for them at our design school, where we worked, in different cabinets in various offices and storage rooms; at home in multiple backpacks and closets; others must be in his studio at our farm which was in a whole different state. Ron stalled for months because he didn't want to confess to her that he couldn't find them all. Eventually, he collected every single one of the micro cassettes and, one Friday afternoon after softball practice, presented them to her in one of my large purses, which was navy blue with flowers embroidered on one side.

She spent most of the weekend holed up in her room watching videos played on the small screen of the video camera because, unfortunately, the cable that connected the camera to the TV had gone missing years ago. Frequently, she would jump up to find Ron or me and share a memory she thought we would enjoy. Late Sunday afternoon, her boyfriend, Cesar, stopped by and was roped into watching "Little Olya" videos. They sat head-to-head over the little screen for a couple of hours before he escaped and went home.

She was still watching videos when I went to bed Sunday night. When she was young, I would tuck Olya in each night. Now, she was 18, and my bedtime was usually before hers. As I lay in bed with Ron watching TV, Olya came in and gave me a hug good night, like she was tucking me in. She talked for a minute, leaned down and gave me another big hug, talked a bit more and then gave me a THIRD hug. Olya had never been a super cuddly person, so this display of affection was unusual for her. I wondered if seeing moments from her childhood had brought out this sentimentality.

The next Friday, I had business meetings in New York City and had invited Olya to go with me. When work was over, we would have a mother-daughter weekend with sightseeing, a Broadway show, shopping, and dinner at an authentic Ukrainian restaurant. Saturday, as we walked across the Brooklyn Bridge on our way to Ground Zero, we talked. I was curious about her feelings about the videos, so I asked, "Did you see anything in the videos that you didn't remember?" She said, "No. I remembered everything. I just never realized how much you played with me. How much time you spent with me. Watching the videos made me appreciate you and Dad even more."

Olya and me on the Brooklyn Bridge.

58. Dust Gray

(Andry's story)

The conversations when I call to talk to Maria and Hannah are always me telling them something about my life in Miami and asking them questions about the village, neighbors, house, ducks, pigs, garden, weather... Having a conversation with them is challenging for me because they both answer "nothing new" to almost everything I ask. If I had been raised by them, it would be a lot harder for me to express my ideas and feelings. I would have been the same way they are, not open or expressive. They live day by day, not thinking about the past or planning for the future. I didn't think Hannah really cared very much about us children, so I was surprised when she said she wanted to see Olya and Dima before she died.

During the summer when I was 16, Hannah got her wish. My mom took Olya and me back to Ukraine to visit for a week. It was the only time I remember Hannah getting excited. She didn't know how to show her joy. She just sat on the bench next to the front door and watched Olya. Her facial expression never changed, but I would occasionally see tears of joy run down her face. Maria got exasperated and said over her shoulder, "Stop getting so emotional. Olya just got here. She isn't leaving yet." But tears aren't just for goodbyes.

Like Hannah, the village she had lived in her whole life had gotten old. The Soviet Union collapsed in 1989, a few years before I was born, but the village didn't totally shut down until I was about six. Most of the younger villagers moved to the city in search of jobs. The villagers that remained were left to cope without a source of income. Over the years, they salvaged the doors, rafters, metal roofing, fencing, and other pieces of the kolhosp to repair their own houses. Now, the only action you see at the kolhosp is the wind moving dried grass around. The village is only good for old people, but when Hannah and the other babushkas were young, the village was bustling. There were lots of families, and everyone was employed doing something at the collective farm. When Maria grew up, she got a job at the kolhosp, where Hannah had also worked. I remember going with Maria to the buildings where hundreds of cows were milked daily. She was in charge of 50 and milked them by attaching tubes to the cow's teats. There were two rows of cows in each of the four buildings. Down the middle of each building was a driveway for a two-horse wagon to deliver hay to each cow's trough. After school, I would go feed extra hay to my favorite cows, get free milk and see what Maria was doing.

Sometimes, in the evenings, I would go out exploring, looking for something to steal. When I started on my adventure, I never knew where I would end up. During summer, I didn't mind a long walk home late at night, but winters there are cold.

So far in my life, Ukraine is the coldest place I have ever been. As a kid, I had a fantasy about building a house in the deep snow, but I didn't have clothes for that type of winter; no gloves, warm coats, or boots. I only wore sneakers. If I was far from home, I would spend the night anywhere I could find shelter that I wouldn't get kicked out of. A few times, I slept at the kolhosp in the hay that was piled by the thick wooden doors waiting to be used for cow bedding. Sleeping in the hay was still cold but better than the 20-minute walk home in the black, 18-degree night. In the mornings, when I woke and looked at the windows, ice crystals would have formed drawings on the glass. I remember wondering, "How did that happen?"

When Maria was away, Hannah was supposed to take care of us. She would lock us inside the house with her, but she spent most of her time sleeping and taking shots of homemade vodka that she bought from the neighbors. In the afternoon, when I was supposed to be taking a nap, I would lie on the bed and stare at the alphabet poster on the wall and try to learn the letters. Sometimes, I would sneak out. I didn't associate Hannah with being my grandmother. She was someone who lived with us. There wasn't anything special about her. She was gray.

I often see people in colors. When I look at Babusha, the woman I really consider my grandmother, my mom's mom, she is purple. Purple is not a bland color. Babusha can be silly and full of herself, but her purple is an owl kind of color. She is also proper and wise. You have to be very polite around her and always say thank you, or she will judge you. Nelson, a friend of mine, is also purple, but they are different shades, and they don't have the same traits.

Olya is lime green. She is blonde and beautiful and stands out, but she can also be sour. Maybe that's just a phase because she's a teenager. My mother is orange. Orange is a happy color but is more long-lasting than purple. She is the kind of person that if you put her anywhere on the map, she will get along and stand out. You can have white, black, and orange walls next to each other, but they would all go together. Orange goes with anything. Dad is brown. He makes brown cool. You don't think of brown as a cool color. It's an older color, but he gives it a fresh look. It's the color of wood. It fits him exactly since he does so much carpentry. In order to be a brown color, you have to know a lot and stand for something. He doesn't care what people think. He isn't afraid to be different. That's how he's always been. He makes being different cool.

The people I am close to have colors. They own their own colors. If a person is yellow and I don't agree, I won't get along with them. They are trying to be someone that it isn't them. They aren't being true to who they are. Nikolai doesn't have a color. What's funny is that Maria is exactly the same color as Hannah, gray. She doesn't show signs of being happy or unhappy. She is quiet. She is hard to read because she doesn't express herself.

When I got adopted, I hadn't expected to be able to come back to the village and find out more about my past and the people that were around me when I was a child. I had lived in the village for seven years and then was moved to the orphanage, so I didn't know much about my family history. As a child, you don't wonder about the past or how you got here. When I was little, I thought my life was simple and normal. I would go on adventures because I was curious about the things around me. But there is another type of curiosity, a more intelligent kind, that you have to develop as you get older or someone has to show you. My mom taught me to be that type of curious. I knew this trip might be my only chance to find out about my life before, to learn about the past and why things turned out how they did. We thought of things that would be good to know, including things I would try to ask Hannah about.

1. What were your parents' names?

2. What did they do for a living?

3. How did they die?

(My mom wanted Olya and me to know our medical history.)

4. How many children were in your family?

5. Where did you live? When did you move to this house?

6. Who are the people in the pictures hanging on the wall?

7. What was it like growing up in the village?

8. What was it like in the village during WWII?

9. What was it like during the Soviet times?

10. Who is Maria's father? How did you meet him? Is he alive?

11. How did Maria and Nikolai meet?

12. Did you like him?

I asked Hannah if we could video her answering questions about her life, and she agreed. My mom would read aloud one of our questions in English. Then I translated it to Ukrainian for Hannah, and then translated her answer back to my mom. Our interview with Hannah was different than I had expected. She didn't volunteer a story but answered anything we asked, no matter how personal the question or painful the memory might be. As Hannah gave more answers, the interview became more intense than I could have ever imagined. Her story was of starvation, murder, alcoholism, rape, and domestic violence. Even though our questions were personal, it was easy to talk to her because she was so honest, open, and unexpectedly coherent.

Hannah is very old, so we assumed she might remember WWII, and we wanted to hear what had happened, how the village had been affected, and what she had personally experienced. She remembered German soldiers walking down the street in front of the house. The soldiers made a fuss over her little sister, Hallah, who was a beautiful toddler. After that, she hid Hallah if soldiers were nearby.

I didn't know that the last name I was born with, Burlaka, had a meaning. It's Russian, and means someone who carries a heavy burden. I learned that Hannah's parents had built the house I had lived in, and she and Maria still lived in it.

I was surprised that Hannah had so much in her and that it was never shared with anyone. Maria didn't even know half of it. Why hadn't Hannah shared? Maybe no one asked her. Maybe there was never someone around that was interested in listening. I think Hannah had wanted to tell her stories to me.

Now I understood why Hannah was dust gray. She and I were sitting on the bench next to the tulips Maria had planted. My mom and I had picked that spot because it would be a nice scene for the video. Ten feet behind Hannah was the picket fence she shared with the neighbor who had killed her mother. What Hannah had described to us in those 30 minutes was too much to handle. Even though it was a sunny summer day, I felt a huge, heavy cloud around our conversation that the camera couldn't capture.

This photo was taken in 2006, outside the Ukrainian courthouse a few minutes after I officially became part of the Seichrist family. Pictured Dad, me, Olya, Mom, and Yelana, our translator.

Epilogue

Andry and I started writing these stories when he was 13, and we sporadically wrote more over the next four years. His high school creative writing teacher loved him and submitted two of his stories to a national writing competition. Andry won second place. Then the stories sat. Years went by.

When Andry was 25, Hannah passed away at 84. She is buried near her parents in the village cemetery the kids and I had visited when Andry was 16 and Olya 13. A year later, when Andry was a copywriting intern at an ad agency in New York, Maria called to tell him that Nikoli had died of Tuberculosis and Cirrhosis of the liver. When I told Olya her biological father had died, her response was, "Good riddance."

Two years later, on February 26, 2021, Olya's boyfriend, Rob, proposed while they were vacationing in Mexico. Prior to the trip, Rob had called Ron and me to ask for our blessing. We were thrilled because, over the two years they had dated, we had seen what great partners they were for each other.

When Olya and I started planning her May wedding, Olya asked if she could invite Maria. Friends were surprised that I had said, "Yes." They asked if I would be jealous and worried that Maria would complicate the wedding. I knew she wouldn't. Maria would be careful and grateful for the chance to see her daughter, our daughter, get married.

Olya is not close to Maria. They don't speak the same language or communicate beyond the occasional shared photo or meme on Instagram... or Maria asking for money, but Olya is empathetic. She said, "I'm Maria's only daughter. This is a day every mother wants to see, and if possible, I would like her to be there." Olya wanted Maria at the wedding not because it was important to her but because she thought it would be meaningful to Maria.

Maria was excited to be invited to the wedding. Andry did the asking since he still speaks Ukrainian. Then he and I worked with Maria to figure out how to get her to the U.S. We sent money so she could travel to Kiev and get her passport and visa. Before I bought her plane tickets, Andry double-checked the travel dates with her. In the end, she was reluctant to come to the U.S. because one of her goats was giving birth around the time of the wedding. Then, on February 24, 2022, Russia invaded Ukraine. Travel to the U.S. became impossible.

Olya and Andry's biological brother, Dima, and the Spanish couple who adopted him came to the wedding. His parents are wonderful people. Even though there is a language barrier, Ron and I have always felt very close to them. Like us, it was important to Cristina and Jamie for the kids to have a relationship. At first, Olya and Dima exchanged phone calls, letters, and photos. When Dima was seven and first saw a photo of Olya with Ron and me, he asked his parents if they would dye their hair blonde so they looked like him. (Ron and I are blonde like Olya.) Each family would also visit the other in Zaragoza or Miami. Once we adopted Andry, the relationship between the three of them got closer. Since Andry is fluent in English and Spanish, communicating was easier. Once they were older, the kids flew on their own to visit the other family for longer stays.

The wedding procession was the Ukrainian national anthem. The flowers were sunflowers, the Ukrainian national flower. In the meantime, the news on TV about Ukraine was horrendous. Andry was still in touch with many of his friends from the orphanage in Bucha. The orphanage was bombed by the Russians because they mistook a WWII-era tank that was a memorial in front of the orphanage as an active tank. Ron and I had taken photos of the kids playing on the tank when we had gone to adopt Andry 15 years earlier. Some of his friends had joined the conflict. Roman was sent to Mariupol, a city that was leveled by the Russians, and he hasn't been heard from since. Another friend is married and has two children. His father-in-law was building them a house in Boryspil when a Russian column came rolling down the street. He looked out the window to see what the noise was and was shot on-site. Because they had been adopted, these weren't our children's stories.

One of my favorite wedding photos is of Olya flanked on each side by a brother. I wonder if the three know how close they came to never seeing each other again. When Ron and I first decided we needed to try to find Dima and Andreshka, as Olya called Andry, we had no idea what to do. It took a million little miracles and thoughtful people to make it happen. At the wedding, Andry, Dima, and Olya (and Rob) vowed that, when possible, they would visit Ukraine together.

At the time of this writing, Maria's small village is still untouched. She has water from the well, and the electricity is on. She has plenty of firewood, grows her own vegetables, has milk from her goats, eggs from her chickens and still decorates eggs in the traditional way. Today, she sent me pictures of some very pretty Pysanky she had put in the mail. We'll get them in a few weeks.

Andry's friends, as boys, playing on the WWII era tank that was a war memorial in front of their orphanage in Bucha. The tank and the orphanage were destroyed by the Russians in 2022.

Andry, Dima and Olya in 2004 in Fuengirola, Spain. This was the first time the three had been together in seven years.

Andry, Olya, and Dima in 2022 reunited, at the family farm for Olya's wedding in Clayton, Georgia.

Acknowledgments

I may never have had the courage to adopt an older child if it hadn't been for a phone call with Deanna McClean. She told me about the five-year-old boy she and her husband had adopted from Bulgaria 14 years earlier. Once a week, until he was proficient in English, she called a translator so her son could ask her questions he hadn't been able to express. One question was if bears lived in the park near their apartment in Chicago. He was relieved to hear Lincoln Park was bear-free. The half-hour conversation I had with Deanna gave me the reassurance I needed to go ahead and submit our adoption application.

Thank you to my husband, Ron. When I married him, he already had six children who, except for one, were grown and out on their own. Somehow, Ron thought getting back on the Merry-go-round with a seventh and eighth child sounded like something he was up for. He has been an amazing partner.

Thank you to Lauren and Michael Gold. Through your questions, you showed me that people wanted to know our story of adopting older children. Now, there are two more Ukrainian siblings, Nastia and Sasha, who have been reunited and call you Mom and Dad.

Thank you to some of my favorite students, Kim Sagami, Anne Lac, Bahareh Batavia, and Christine Call, who acted as nannies and cycled through Olya's elementary school years. You all did a terrific job of helping with homework and playing with her. The daily notes you left detailing special moments you knew I would be sad to have missed are so precious to me. I saved every note, and a couple of your anecdotes are in the book.

Thank you to Larry Gordon, a hoodie-wearing copywriting student whom Andry looked up to. Larry was a great role model and taught Andry that Rap isn't the only acceptable music genre, that Opera is beautiful, and that Country has outstanding lyrics and storylines.

Thank you to Kristin Murphy, my assistant, who was the older sister and wise voice Olya, Andry, or I sometimes needed.

Thank you to the excellent teachers who saw the potential in my children and the unique needs they had, especially Denise Formosa for finding ways to make an overwhelmed 6-year-old feel comfortable; Rachel Unger for modifying spelling tests until Olya could master the words and develop confidence; and Jen Karetnick for seeing Andry's writing ability and convincing him he had talent.

Thank you to Cheryl, Erik, Rolf, and Tony, Ron's older children, for taking care of our dogs when we had to travel to Ukraine for too many weeks, for helping at kiddie birthday parties, for thoughtful Christmas presents, for teasing, life advice and all the other brotherly and sisterly things you did for Olya and Andry to make them feel like part of the pack.

Thank you to Bonnie Lunt for your 30-year friendship. Your recommendation letters were part of our adoption dossiers. Your words married Olya and Rob. If something had happened to Ron and me before the kids grew up, we know you would have been there for them.

And thank you, as always, to my parents, Cara and Jim Boyd. You demonstrated to me every day of my life what it takes to be a great parent. You were present and involved in my life; you listened, understood, and told me you loved me. The very few times you weren't perfect, you had the strength of character to say you were sorry. Like you were there for me, you have always been there for your grandchildren, Olya and Andry.

Denise Formoso, Olya's 2nd grade teacher, Olya and Pippa, Halloween 2003.

Andry, Olya, and the cats, Birthday and Tuesday, visiting their grandparents, Jim and Cara Boyd, at their house in Indialantic, Florida in 2008.

Andry, Olya, Ron, and me in 2006. Ron was a wonderful, enthusiastic parent partner who enjoyed the children as much as I did.

About the Authors

Pippa Seichrist started her career as an art director, and worked at several ad agencies before going on to found, with her husband, the most award-winning school in the world for advertising and design. The single school they started grew into a network of 15 schools in eight countries. Pippa enjoys creating almost anything from pottery, to furniture, to events. You can find her dog face jugs in several folk art galleries, or search online for Dog Face Pottery. Most recently she turned the family's historic property, Satolah Creek Farm, in the mountains of north Georgia, into a magical place for farm stays, weddings, and events.

Andry Seichrist started his career as a copywriter and interned and worked at ad agencies in New York, Spain, Miami and Atlanta. He decided to follow his entrepreneurial spirit and started a company in Highlands, NC, that helps homeowners bring their remodeling and landscaping projects to life.

The cover image is of
Olya's hands holding
one of Maria's eggs
that broke in the mail.

Made in the USA
Columbia, SC
29 October 2024

fdf083c4-8d6c-47c8-be46-bff321f86b7eR01